ZEN

A WAY OF LIFE

Christmas Humphreys was born in 1901 and followed his father, Sir Travers Humphreys, into the criminal law, becoming a QC and spending the last ten years of his career as a permanent judge at the Central Criminal Court. While at Cambridge, he found Theosophy and then Buddhism, and in 1924 with his wife founded the Buddhist Lodge of The Sophical Society. This, as the Buddhist Society, London, is now the oldest and largest Buddhist organisation in Europe. He wrote many works on Buddhism and Zen, and was chosen to represent British Buddhism at the Thanksgiving Service held in St Paul's Cathedral in 1977. He died in 1983.

TEACH YOURSELF BOOKS

ZEN

A WAY OF LIFE

Christmas Humphreys

TEACH YOURSELF BOOKS

Hodder and Stoughton

First printed 1962
Seventh impression 1981
Reissued in this format 1985

ISBN 0 340 38484 0

Printed and bound in Great Britain for
Hodder and Stoughton Educational,
a division of Hodder and Stoughton Ltd,
Mill Road, Dunton Green, Sevenoaks, Kent,
by Richard Clay (The Chaucer Press) Ltd,
Bungay, Suffolk.

CONTENTS

ACKNOWLEDGEMENTS

ALL the extracts in Chapters Six and Eleven have been taken from *The Wisdom of Buddhism*, edited by Christmas Humphreys, Michael Joseph, 1960, where the source of each extract is given in full. It is only right, however, that the source be given again here.

In Chapter Six 'The Heart Sutra' is taken from *Buddhist Texts Through the Ages*, ed. Edward Conze. Bruno Cassirer, Oxford, 1954. The same applies to 'The Buddha Nature and the Void'. 'Duality and Non-Duality', 'Suchness', 'The Bodhisattva's Training' and 'The Perfection of Giving' are taken from *Selected Sayings from the Perfection of Wisdom*, trans. Edward Conze. The Buddhist Society, London. 1955. Selections from the Diamond Sutra are taken from *The Diamond Sutra*, trans. A. F. Price. The Buddhist Society, 1947. 'The Zen Unconscious, Suchness and the Middle Way' is taken from *The Zen Doctrine of No-Mind*, D. T. Suzuki, Rider, 1949. 'The Bodhisattva's Nature' is taken from the Siksha-Samuccaya as trans. by Kenneth Saunders in *The Gospel for Asia*, S.P.C.K., 1928. *The Voice of the Silence* was trans. and compiled by H. P. Blavatsky and published by the Theosophical Publishing Co., 1889.

In Chapter Eleven the extracts from Hui-neng are from *The Sutra of Wei Lang (Hui-neng)*, trans. Wong Mou-lam, Luzac, 1944. That from Shen-hui is taken from *Buddhist Texts Through the Ages*, as mentioned above. That from Huang Po is taken from *The Zen Teaching of Huang Po*, trans. John Blofeld, Rider, 1958, and 'On Trust in the Heart' from *Manual of Zen Buddhism*, D. T. Suzuki, Eastern Buddhist Society, 1935.

PREFACE

ZEN, a comprehensive term for the experience of Reality, scarcely comes within the ambit of things to teach yourself, yet as a Way of Life, a system of training for the Zen experience it fits to perfection.

As it happens, I had planned such a work in outline before I was asked to contribute to this series, and its fourfold object is none the less appropriate here.

1. To check, if possible, the growth in England of anything like the 'Beat Zen' of the U.S.A., where the term Zen, with little if any understanding of its meaning, has been adopted by certain lost, unhappy minds of the younger generation to express their own subconscious fears and longings, and to give them a rational excuse for mental and moral misbehaviour.

2. To consider again the problems raised in my *Zen Comes West*, and to provide a possible solution. For if success in Zen, at least in the later stages of training, needs a qualified Zen master, and none is available in Europe, what can Zen students, numbering now many hundreds, possibly thousands, do about it? Here at least is one solution, based on the ancient maxim, 'When the pupil is ready the master appears'.

3. To emphasize, and indeed to press home the truth, that Zen is the reward of considerable study, self-discipline and mind-development. It cannot be achieved with a smattering of reading, a gift for the absurd, and a discarding of all mental and moral standards.

4. To suggest, as the fruit of long experience, that the best way to approach the 'moment' of Zen is through Zen Buddhism, which is but one school of Mahayana Buddhism, which is itself a complementary expansion of the Theravada School of Buddhism, which is itself a field of thought and teaching

built up round the understanding by his disciples of the Teaching of Gautama Buddha, the All-Enlightened, All-Compassionate One. In other words, to advocate beginning at the beginning, which is still a necessity in the mastery of any art or craft, physical or mental or spiritual, whatsoever.

Hence the plan of this book. First a thorough grounding in the principles of the earliest school of Buddhism, the Theravada, or teaching of the Elders. Only when the mind has come to terms with this radically different way of life is it useful to expand into the wider but complementary field of the Mahayana, 'the great vehicle (of salvation)' in which may be found some of the noblest attainments of the human heart and mind. Selected Scriptures from this mighty field of thought will give the student the 'perfume' of its teaching in its distilled intensity. Then, and in my view then alone, is the mind in a fit state to consider the famous Zen School of Japan, its history, unique form of teaching, and the Scriptures which are used in training the student to pass beyond the limitations of literature in any form.

With this doctrinal background, and assuming the changes which such study produces in the student mind, the field is ploughed for the seed of Zen. This stage will be soon enough to consider its nature and meaning, and how it may be found; to enter the realm of teasing paradox, and to see why nothing truthful can in fact be said of Zen. For here words fail. 'The rest is silence, and a finger pointing the Way.'

Yet I believe that the man or woman of strong will and balanced mind can, by self-training, travel far towards the goal at which that finger points. And my belief is based on thirty years' experience of such training, applied to myself and to those who thought that I could help them to their own experience.

Hence this book, a humble offering from a Western mind to fellow Westerners who share the view that Zen is neither of East nor West but that any man, in any time and place, can at least begin – to 'teach himself Zen'.

I am most grateful to all who have fair-copied the amateurish mess in which my writing first appears on a patient and ill-used machine. To Mrs. Mary Anthony, Mrs. Constance Jones, Mrs. Monica Hyde and Mrs. Joyce Armstrong I bow in gratitude, and to Miss Agnes Iron of Dover for patient work in the creation of the Glossary. As all its terms have been taken, though often considerably modified, from *A Popular Buddhist Dictionary*, published by the Arco Press, I here confess my borrowing from this, my own much larger Glossary. The Bibliography, designed for students of Buddhism specially interested in Zen, is based on the Reading List supplied by the Buddhist Society, London. The Ten Principles of Zen, used by way of Conclusion, first appeared in the May 1961 issue of *The Middle Way*, the Journal of the Society, and I am grateful to Mrs. M. H. Robins, its Editor, for permission to reprint.

Finally, I make my Zen bow to my wife, co-founder of the Buddhist Society in 1924, as of its Zen Class in 1930, and Mrs. Martha Vaughan, one of its present teachers, for their views and doubts and bright ideas in the preparation of this book which, the latest venture in the field of Zen Buddhism, may have stepped a foot or two into the field of Zen.

T. C. H.

St. John's Wood,
January 1962

INTRODUCTION

ANY man can begin to teach himself Zen, but he is not likely to be very successful unless he already possesses at least some measure of the following qualities:

(1) He must want It, whatever he thinks 'It' is, enormously, as an actual spiritual experience of Reality, want it as badly as a man whose head is held under water wants air. Zen is not a form of 'fun and games' for those of light intellect and ready wit. It is a whole-time task for the total man, for its ultimate Goal is no less than Buddhahood.

(2) He must possess humility which is yet consistent with a powerful will bent to a clearly perceived end. For the journey to the top of Everest begins at the bottom, and between the two lie immense difficulties and perhaps long periods of time.

(3) He must have faith, which will be sorely tried at times, in the truth of at least three statements of fact. First, that the Buddha attained Enlightenment; secondly, that this Enlightenment is a state of mind already possessed by all men; and, thirdly, that a Way exists by which each man may become aware of his own Enlightenment. Within this minimum of faith, and Buddhism calls for no more, he must develop the power to 'walk on' unceasingly, through a brick wall or over a precipice if need be, but never stopping for one instant until the Goal is reached.

(4) He must have a mind of his own and some control of it. Until the power of thought is considerably developed it will not be possible to reach its limits; yet only when the limits are reached can thought be consciously abandoned, and No-thought recognized as the ultimate purpose of all thinking. Only in this exalted state does knowledge about Buddhism, about Zen Buddhism and about Zen give way to experience, however brief and insufficient, of that awareness of which

'Buddhism' is the extended product, and Zen but one of a hundred synonyms.

(5) He must be profoundly and actively aware of the limitations of the intellect and conscious of the faculty which supersedes it, the intuition, by which alone the opposites are transcended, by which alone each man will find the subtle Middle Way which is above yet between them all, and KNOW Reality.

(6) He must have a mind sufficiently well balanced to stand without cracking the strain which training for Zen imposes on character. The fanatic, the crank, the man of gravely lopsided development, the man whose outward life is a mask above a seething cauldron of repressed desires and ambitions, all these are warned off the field of Zen, for the mental homes of the U.S.A. and Europe know them all too well. In the same way those who seek to use Zen for their own purposes, to prove their own theories or to further their own ideal, will be more than disappointed. They will suffer as all must suffer who use a spiritual power for personal ends.

(7) Finally, this would-be master of Zen must have an innate feeling for Zen which is as difficult to describe as it is unmistakable in practice. It is a lightness of touch, a power and willingness to 'sit loose' to life. It appears as a sense of nonsense, and the power to laugh at all things, first oneself. The man who has no laughter in him, no sense of poetry and song, who cannot dance, at least in heart, to the music of the morning air, is never a man of Zen.

He who has these qualities in some degree may begin to teach himself Zen. But Zen is the flower of Buddhism; beneath it lies a great tree of the developed doctrine, practice and culture of the varied schools of Buddhism; and beneath the tree are the roots of the tree, the basic principles which are common to all schools. It is my belief after forty years' experience that all attempts by Westerners to 'have a go' at Zen in utter ignorance of the background, origin and growth of the Zen School of Buddhism, content with the reading of a few Zen stories and violent efforts to solve a self-chosen *koan* are doomed to failure; perhaps worse, a revulsion from all spiritual endeavour, and possibly grave damage to the mind.

At the outset there are three concepts to be clearly distinguished, Buddhism, Zen Buddhism, and Zen. 'Buddhism' is the vast field of thought and culture built up through the centuries about the teaching of the Buddha, which was in turn the expression, or partial expression of his Enlightenment. It has two main schools, the earlier *Theravada*, the Teaching of the Elders, and the later *Mahayana*, or Great Career. 'Zen Buddhism' is a school of the Mahayana founded in China in the sixth century A.D., and later transferred to Japan where it flourishes today. It aims at direct approach to Enlightenment, and is unique as such. 'Zen' has at least three meanings. First, as the Japanese version of the Chinese Ch'an, which is in turn derived from the Sanskrit Dhyana, meaning – though no one English word suffices – deep meditation. Hence the 'Zen' school of Buddhism, sometimes called in early works the Meditation School. This is the lowest meaning of the term. The highest is yet another name for the nameless THAT, the ultimate Absolute which is beyond all names. The middle meaning, and that which the word implies for the most part of this book is the mystical experience of THAT, a flash of awareness, out of time and beyond the limitations of personal consciousness, of the Ultimate from which all the world we know has derived. It is in this sense that we speak of a touch of Zen, or Zen experience. In Japan it is known as *Satori*, or in the Soto school as *Kensho*, a 'first showing'. As an experience this is not the same as Enlightenment, and may be removed from it by very long periods of training. Hence the saying that Satori is not the goal of Zen but rather the opening of the Zen path which leads in time – or out of time – to the end of self as we understand it. But whatever name be used for this experience, mystics of all ages have described it in their own language by analogy, symbol and glyph. It is the 'inspiration' of genius, the 'grace' of the deeper religious life, the vision of the great thinker, musician, poet, or worker for mankind who, having got It, strives to express it.

Satori is not confined to Zen Buddhism, as shown in a hundred examples by R. H. Blyth in his *Zen in English Literature*, but it is a strange fact in religious history that the Zen School of Buddhism is the only one in which the mind is deliberately trained to achieve it. True, in one sense no mere training is enough. Philosophers can miss it utterly; few psychologists lift their eyes to where it dwells, and saints can fall far short of it; for all these move and have their being in a world of duality, whereas Zen training is designed to break through to Non-duality. This is the sole and only purpose of all Zen effort, and the effort must come from within. Fellow seekers and – with far greater skill – Zen masters will help to point the seeker in the right direction, but when all this help is given, the road of Zen is a road of 'Do it yourself' – teach *yourself* Zen!

I believe in Rebirth, and that Zen training is only usefully attempted with the aid of this doctrine. In one life a man may make brief contact with this inner world, by religion, philosophy or some other Way, and then drift away because the will to achieve is insufficient to hold the contact. In the next or a later life he may renew the contact, and perhaps go further in his study – and then weary of the search in favour of some new interest. But the light, being seen, can never be utterly ignored, even though the glimpse was truly 'as through a glass darkly'. Sooner or later the real study begins, and in the life in which this happens it will explain the type of mind which, the moment it hears of Zen, or the equivalent of mystical experience, will know beyond all argument that this is what it wants, and wants very badly. Surely those who thus accept the difficult teaching at sight, and will not be put off their new and intense inquiry, knew it of old; henceforth easier to classify the members of a class or group in search of Zen. Some will drift away for that life; some go and come back; some find it.

What, then, of those who achieve a high degree of experience apparently without previous Zen training? The answer surely lies in this doctrine of rebirth. The fortunate ones had had their training, possibly lives of it, in days gone by. Now they were ripe for the break-through. Even then, however, in the cases of which we have personal knowledge, there was a desperate inward searching, a tension in the deeps of mind, and the experience was the correspondingly intense release. But even these experiences are but the raw material of mystical progress. There must be the ratification, the translation into rational terms, and the slow 'maturing' of the experience into character. These latter phases need guidance by an expert hand, but there is an old saying, 'When the pupil is ready the Master appears.'

Meanwhile hundreds, perhaps thousands of Westerners are seeking Zen. Who are they? They may, it seems, be classified as follows:

(1) The majority seek a Saviour, whether they know it consciously or not. They hope to find in Zen what they have sought in vain elsewhere, Someone to do the work for them, to 'save them from their sins'. To them Zen has nothing to say.

(2) There are those who seek and play with anything new, to titillate the intellectual and emotional fancy. They come, but soon they go; Zen is much too hard work for them.

(3) There are those who seek something, they know not what, to fill the void within the mind which seeks for *some* explanation of life and a working plan for living according to its purpose.

(4) There are those in particular, light of touch, who seek a way which, while profound as need be, allows for the impish, irrational element in the mind which is unallowed for in other Ways. But many of these overdo the element of wit, and are the psychological parents of 'Beat' Zen, as practised, so we are told, in the U.S.A.

Finally, there are those who at the first contact shout, '*That's* what I've always wanted', and find that there is no longer question of the pursuit of Zen; Zen is pursuing them.

Of these, the third group will find that Buddhism helps them, but probably not yet Zen Buddhism. Many of the fourth group will stay the course, and those few in the fifth group would not be able to let go even if they wished to do so. For these alone are seeking Zen in its own home, on its own plane of Non-duality, and do not attempt to drag it down to their own level of the intellect or worse. These are the pioneer few on whom lies the responsibility of finding a middle way between 'Square' and 'Beat' Zen, between the classical tradition of China and Japan and an entirely new form which utterly ignores it.

What, then, is the training? None has ever been laid down in China or Japan, and none yet suggested for the Western mind. But the history of Zen Buddhism contains the slow formulation of two divergent methods of preparing the pupil for his first Zen 'experience', to be found respectively in the Rinzai branch and the Soto branch of Japanese Zen. Here, for reasons to be given more fully later, we are concerned with Rinzai Zen. But long before this division took place the Zen Masters who followed the tradition of Bodhidharma from the sixth to the eighth century in China needed no system of training at all. They were men of colossal minds and great achievement, and they taught their pupils as the pupil had need. Only when the standard of achievement declined did later masters resort to the collected Sayings of their spiritual ancestors, and develop the famous methods, used today, of the Koan and Mondo. But even these need a qualified master, or *Roshi*, to supervise their use with safety and success, and we in the West, in the absence of Zen masters, must find our own way to prepare for Zen experience, either while waiting for expert help from the East, or without waiting for it. The problem is already acute, as I have explained in *Zen Comes West* (1960), where the whole situation is reviewed. But whatever the help afforded by the Roshis of Japan, it is surely obvious that the West, knowing its own mental make-up, must work out its own preliminary training and prepare it from the ground up.

Here are some suggested guiding principles. First, we must approach the whole field of Buddhism as it were from the top, from the viewpoint of that which gave it birth, the Buddha's Enlightenment. A student approaches most aspects of Buddhism in terms of principles, theories, doctrines, each embedded in words which are themselves translated from a foreign language. But the seeker of Zen is not concerned with doctrines, and much less with words, save as they express and help him to achieve the Buddha's Enlightenment. He is concerned with 'getting it' and not with 'knowing about it', save as the latter is necessary for the former. In his study of the basic doctrines of Buddhism, the roots of the tree of which Zen is the flower, he will remember at all times that doctrine is the expression of Enlightenment; it does not produce it! In the same way he will study the expanded principles of the Mahayana because here the whole plane of consciousness is lifted, and many of its Scriptures go as far as words may go in expressing the actual experience of Zen. But again, fascinating though this exalted field of metaphysics and mystical philosophy may be, it can be a snare to the feet of the pilgrim unless he firmly uses it for his one sole purpose, to help him on the way to his own and the world's enlightenment. In the same way, even when the study of Zen Buddhism, as the flowering of Mahayana, is begun, nothing concerning it must give the student pause save as it arms and prepares him for the final assault on his spiritual Everest. Yet a study of the history of Zen as a school is of profound importance, and a great deal can be learnt from it. The genesis of the school, the Chinese reaction to Indian Buddhism, the assimilation of the latter in the Chinese mind with profound change of emphasis and technique, the lives of the Patriarchs and what Zen meant to them, how they taught and whom and when, all this is more than helpful, it is necessary for the right formulation of the Western school of Zen. In the same way the arising and possible decline by codification of the Koan technique, the distinction of the 'gradual' and 'sudden' schools of Soto and Rinzai, and the apparent cause of the 'Beat' Zen movement in the U.S.A. – all this is potentially helpful. Only then does it become of interest and importance to analyse the history of Zen in Europe, the work of Dr. D. T. Suzuki and his Western followers, and the present problem of Zen for the West. For the reader of this book is part of it; he is helping to create the problem and must help to solve it. What follows is therefore a tentative outline of self-training, as preparation for Zen experience. For there is no Way which leads direct to Satori, and not even a Master can do more than point the seeker in the right direction. 'Even Buddhas do but point the Way.'

The training is mental, in that it all takes place within the mind, which we know is All-Mind, which is No-Mind, or Mind-Only, and to the Buddhist nothing exists that is not first born in the mind which is part of Mind.

The process is dual, the understanding and assimilation of doctrine, and the development of powers of character. By doctrine is meant those principles which form the basis of what the West calls Buddhism. But these are forces, not interesting theories. Karma, if true, is a law of the universe, perhaps the greatest law; the fact of change, when applied by the individual remorselessly, can profoundly affect his actions as well as his state of mind; the fact of suffering and the way to remove it is in a sense the bedrock of Buddhism. As for character, this is the man, and every spiritual power (let us eschew the outmoded 'virtue'), must be developed sooner or later to the full, as every weakness – and what else is vice? – be eliminated before the attainment of the goal.

We surely begin with a survey of the situation within. What now is my state of mind? What powers and faculties have I, and what inhibits their best use? What do I lack of needful qualities and what do I know of the unconscious mind and its power to order my thoughts and actions unknown to 'me'? Thereafter we get to work, and the process is surely twofold, to pull down the old building and to build the new. We cannot successfully superimpose a new habit and direction of thought on existing habits now believed to be adequate. Negatively, we must slowly remove outmoded concepts; for example, that of God as an immortal Saviour of my soul, of the limitation of spiritual progress to the brief moments of one life, of the absolute distinction of good and evil, pleasant and unpleasant, as applied to all situations by dogmatic thinking. We must analyse the thing called self and see its falsity, withdraw at least some of the projections by which we blame everything about us for consequences we ourselves have caused, and we must remove from circumstance its power to dominate our lives. Yet this is but half the story. Thereafter, though in a sense at the same time, we must build up the needful powers of indomitable will – in common parlance 'guts' – the inflexible will to achieve which knows no stopping. We must develop the intuition, the power which alone will enable us at last to break through the ceiling of thought into Reality; we must cultivate even in thought that lightness of touch whose supreme ideal is to 'let the mind abide nowhere'. All this itself needs patience and humility, but we shall not get far on the road to Zen, nor use what we get in a way which will gain us more, without these qualities. Only then can we look at long last and with fresh eyes at Zen. What is it? How can we find what we have, and live as what we are, enlightened ones that have no need for Zen? At least we shall be considering these questions half-way up the mountain at the top of which lies the answer. Only then shall we deserve Zen, having earned it.

From this brief précis it should be clear that Zen is not for the religious play-boy. It is not an activity which can be added to other spiritual ways of life, still less can it be achieved by occasional periods of attention 'as time permits'. Zen is a task for twenty-four hours a day, and in each moment of the day is opportunity for finding it. It will not be found by 'fun and games', nor in bursts of brilliant paradox, yet it may be that it can be found without spending ten years in a Japanese monastery. We believe that he who wants Zen and nothing less, who has or is prepared to develop the qualities of mind and character needed for the great adventure, he will achieve. None can help him greatly, in England or Japan, but no power on earth can stay him from success. The wisdom of the past, the precepts of the masters, the technique of the schools of Zen extant today, all these are at his service. But to succeed, he must teach *himself* Zen!

PART ONE

BUDDHISM

CHAPTER ONE

THE BUDDHA AND HIS ENLIGHTENMENT

THE Buddha was a man, by name Gautama Siddhartha, but his place in the spiritual history of mankind is shown by the title which he earned and by which he is known to the world. He became, by effort intensely applied for countless incarnations, *Buddha*, the Enlightened One. In the esoteric tradition there are grades of spiritual achievement, and a hierarchy of those who on earth have attained liberation from the Wheel of Becoming. These self-perfected men, pilgrims who have reached the goal of Nirvana, are known to mankind by many names; Buddhists call them Arhats and Bodhisattvas. But whether described by their Buddhist names, or as Rishis, Mahatmas, the Brothers, or the Masters, their spiritual status is inconceivably higher than our own; yet they, according to the timeless and unwritten records of the East, acknowledge the Buddha as 'the Patron of the Adepts', their Master and Lord.

What, then, would be the depth of our humility of mind in the presence of such men made perfect, and even more so in the aura of the Sambuddha, Lord of them all. We must use imagination to bridge the gap that separates their vast achievement from our own. Let us think of an all-wise friend with the largest mind, the deepest heart of understanding, the widest vision of the world and the cosmic processes of world- and man-becoming. There are such men in the world of men, though they are rare indeed. If they are not met their words may be known in writings or recorded speech, and our petty minds can glimpse the glory of theirs by such a means.

Now let us think of a mind so purified, expanded and ennobled in its range of vision, and realize that such a man is at most the disciple of one of the Great Ones still in a physical body. As such he is still far from the spiritual grandeur which they have achieved. And these Great Ones call the Buddha Master. . . .

Such men, in high or low degree, are living expressions of love and strength and purity, and the whole range of noble attributes with which we adorn those pilgrims of the Way who have reached the 'further shore'. Theirs is the vision of the Whole, achieved by countless lives of 'right effort' in the elimination of self and the expansion of the selfless Self which moves to Enlightenment. In the course of that journey they suffered torments which we cannot yet conceive in tearing the weed of self from the heart of selfishness, until in each the self died before the Self, the personal part before the impersonal whole. The Christ-Buddha-principle broke free of the limitations of the personality, and the 'Thousand-petalled Lotus' was unfolded utterly. Thereafter the gates of Nirvana were opened for one who had earned the right of entry – and he entered not. The supreme sacrifice was made in the full awareness of its implications, and the reward of a thousand lives of endeavour was laid aside for the unending task of enlightening mankind.

The Buddha returned to the world of men to teach Awakening. Buddhas are wakeners, rousing every man who has ears to hear to rise from the sloth of illusion and tread the Way to his own enlightenment. Lack of awakening is the origin of Ill, the cause of suffering, and the only Buddhist 'sin' is that of absence of vision, ignorance. The Wisdom to be gained is a new dimension of consciousness, an awareness, in the words of a Buddhist Scripture, the *Dhammapada*, of 'Self as the lord of self'. The Buddha pointed a Way, and about that Way, and on either side of it, have grown up the Schools and sects of what in the West we know as 'Buddhism'. But, as Dr. Suzuki says, 'the life of Buddhism is the unfolding of the inner spiritual life of the Buddha himself, rather than his exposition of it, recorded as the *Dharma* in Buddhist literature'.*

Essays in Zen Buddhism. First Series. First edn., p. 37.

Thus Buddhism is the life-force which carries forward a spiritual movement called Buddhism. It is therefore strange that Buddhist scholars, in all parts of the world, are often so engrossed in the so-called teachings of the Buddha that they neglect the study of the spiritual experience which gave rise to that Teaching. For Buddhism is a record of Enlightenment and the Way that leads to it; it is the shrine and should be the vehicle of his Enlightenment. Without Enlightenment Gautama would not have become Buddha; because Buddha *is* Buddha, we can study and attempt to apply Buddhism today.

Some men heard the 'lion's Roar of Truth' when he spoke to them in the forest glades of Northern India 2,500 years ago. Some men heard the Message of the Way from these, the supremely fortunate. We in the West read, in translation, what others think they understood of that long tradition of a mighty Message, and in the silence of our meditation hear again the splendour of that Word. 'Thus have I heard . . .', murmurs the Bhikkhu, the Buddhist monk, as he attempts to give in simple language the Dhamma (Teaching) of the All-Enlightened One, and we who hear have the privilege, strenuously earned, to hearken and obey.

The Buddha achieved Enlightenment and taught mankind the Way. Little can usefully be said of his ultimate experience, but much may be written of the Way which leads to it. A thousand thousand men have climbed to the summit of Fuji-Yama in Japan to see the sun rise in the distant sea; none told the same tale of the journey. So we, on the slopes of the mountain of Reality, learn of the Way from those ahead of us, and pass to our younger brothers the wisdom learned. The Way which lies within from its first beginning to its unknown end is, like all else in existence, twofold. From the negative point of view, it is destructive, for a man must clear his building-site of rubbish before he can begin to build. We must break the bonds of desire, the adhesions of ill-thought. We must cleanse the mind of the illusion of discrimination, the sense of separateness which leads us to imagine that 'I am I'.

At the same time, positively, we must learn to expand the Self, until this Wisdom-heart within breaks from the shell of unregenerate self and expands into Enlightenment. Does the dewdrop slip into the Shining Sea, or, as the mystics have described it, is it the Shining Sea which fills the dewdrop with the Plenum-Void? It matters not, for the experience is beyond our wording.

With this expansion all else follows. 'Seek ye first the Kingdom of Heaven, and all things shall be added unto you.' He who begins to achieve enlightenment finds that the lower faculties, sworn though they are in fealty to self, change to a new obedience, and for the first time there is a total man to move to his own salvation.

Enlightenment is perfect understanding, and we can and should begin the process now. A positive effort is needed, and the way to enlightenment is to understand till it hurts. The mind must be stretched to include emotions, thoughts and points of view entirely foreign to the narrow limits of our present life. We must understand the mind of the criminal, lie down in the gutter of thought with the drunken prostitute, the debaucher of children, the scum of the earth, for we shall not rise in consciousness to the level of the saint while feeling separate from the lowest members of our family. He who can enter into the vilest corners of the human mind will purge himself of pride that he is 'not as other men'. Then, and only then, may he reach for the feet of those who do not fear contamination from his grubby hands. To expand the heart to Oneness, and beyond, such is the meaning of Enlightenment, for the Buddha-Mind is one with the Universe, one with the All-Mind from which it came.

But if we cannot now be one with the greatest of our human family, we can induce, by the powerful faculty of imagination, something of the state of consciousness which great expansion brings. We can induce some measure of the cool serenity which comes when the conflict of the opposites, the rival claims of the two sides of the penny, have died away. When all distinctions are glimpsed as falsely imagined, and the essence of 'pennydom' is understood as beyond the use of either of its complementary sides, then something unforgettable has been achieved. The same applies to that sense of certainty, the absence of doubt and tentative experiment which must obtain so long as we let ourselves bᵉ partial and one-sided in our views. We are certain, with a masterly touch in circumstance, or large or small, and in all action we feel some dim yet growing awareness of that rhythm of life which is the universal process working through its pure or impure medium, you and me.

The results of even this exercise in self-enlightening are proof that our chosen road is 'right'. Henceforth we ask ourselves, not how much time and energy should be given to the Way, but *what else matters* – save increased awakening? Does this or that lead, or does it not, to further enlightenment? This is the new criterion of action, the sole excuse and reason for anything at all.

The ladders to this new state of consciousness are various. Right action is called in India the way of Karma-Yoga; emotion-devotion to the Beloved ideal is the way of Bhakti-Yoga, of the mystic of all ages. The intellect, using the way of Jnana-Yoga, studies the opposites, and attempts to approximate more closely every pair until it can proclaim in triumph, 'Thou *art* THAT'. Only the intuition, the faculty of *Buddhi*, can go further, and it goes so far that it passes beyond our intellectual ken. Here there is no distinction between this and that, nor awareness of any difference. 'Thou' and 'THAT' are no more the ultimates of the part and the whole perceived as one – the difference is extinguished. The intuition functions by direct awareness. It is therefore the faculty of Enlightenment, that in man which frees itself from the last illusion – separateness, and being free it knows that it is free, and is of the substance of Nirvana. If this is to most of us an ideal state beyond imagining, it is not impossible to visualize that nothing less can be the Goal.

The Buddha became, by his own efforts, the Supremely Awakened One. He returned to point out, in the greatest detail, the Path which had led him to that Goal. His Teaching is a Way, the Way to Enlightenment. Then what else matters, what else has the least significance for the pilgrim of that Way but the goal at the end of it, Enlightenment? Henceforth illusion is our only sin, for of illusion, or ignorance, is born the folly of our lust. Believing self to be in some way different from other selves we crave for self, and cause our suffering. In the illusion of separation we hate the fellow aspects of our Self. Unknowing Self to be a flame of the light of Enlightenment, we cling to the spiritual pride which holds this awakening Self superior to other Selves that seem not yet awakened. All this is folly, a cloud which hides the Light, an obstruction on the Way. How much do we *want* to remove the obstruction, to unveil the Light? As much as a man whose head is held below water craves for air? As much as a man in love wants life? When the whole soul's will is bent upon the Way, when the passion to achieve the next step on the Path consumes all other desire, then only are we worthy of the label 'Buddhist', for then only shall we move direct to the heart of 'Buddhism', that utter and serene Enlightenment which the All-Compassionate One achieved and offered to mankind.

What, then, is Nirvana, this State of Enlightenment? Does it very much matter? I do not believe a student who says, 'I shall not begin the journey until I fully understand the nature of the end.' Do climbers at the foot of the mountain refuse to begin the ascent until they know in detail the nature of the summit and the view to be obtained? Surely it is better to move to the more, the better, without arguing, in the absence of all direct evidence, the nature of the Most, the Best? For we have no evidence about Nirvana which is at present for us direct. All we know, and all that any man who has not reached the Goal can know, is expressed by Sir Edwin Arnold in the eighth book of the *Light of Asia*:

> 'If any teach *Nirvana* is to cease,
>   Say unto such they lie.
> If any teach *Nirvana* is to live,
>   Say unto such they err: . . .'

In brief, *Nirvana is*. The rest is silence, and a finger pointing the Way. For the end is, *ex hypothesi*, beyond description. In the words of the Chinese classic, 'The Tao that can be expressed is not the Eternal Tao.' It may be described in negatives, on the ground that all positive statements must be inadequate, yet in the end the final negative is reached, the *Neti, Neti,* 'not this, not this', of Indian philosophy, the *Mu* (No!), of the Zen Master. Does this help our painfully short-sighted minds? But if negative words and positive words are equally futile, if the 'Fulness-Void' and the 'Absolute Reality' are so many noises in the air, what is to be done to improve our understanding? The answer is the Way and the treading of it, for if it is not practised it remains but a collection of words. These words point the way to an inner experience. The words themselves produce nothing; only the practice of the Way will bring that experience, as thousands of our fellow men have testified.

The sole excuse for considering Nirvana at all is that a rational ideal can act as a spur to effort, and that the right frame of mind with a view to the journey's end may help to induce pre-glimpses of its splendour. But intellectual discussion is waste of time, and worse, for it delays the awareness that words, the medium of discussion, must sooner or later be left behind. It is easy to speak of a self that is 'blown out' as a candle is blown out, of a Self which re-becomes the SELF. But these are words, the clothing of concepts, and no substitute for the vast awareness of Nirvana.

Far more important to the Buddhist pilgrim is the tremendous fact that Nirvana is attainable on earth, in this very life and here, wherever here may be, and now, or in some other moment of our illusion, time. More, Nirvana *is* Samsara, and Samsara *is* Nirvana. They are closer than the two sides of a coin; they are two modes of the same experience. In Dr. Suzuki's words, 'There is nothing infinite apart from finite things.' Or as R. H. Blyth has put it, 'Zen is the infinite way of doing finite things.' This sudden jolt to the inquiring mind arrests the Western flight to the Other, the craving to escape from this to That, 'from darkness to Light, from death to Immortality'. There is no such journey, for the dark and the light are both within, both here and now. There is no later, final Heaven, for heaven and hell are another of the pairs of opposites, alike the product of the thinking mind, the effects of a million causes made and modified by every breath we draw.

Meanwhile, we may know, as distinct from knowing about, Nirvana within the present darkness of our minds. There is no such thing as the Great Renunciation save as it is the final flowering of seed perpetually sown. Hour by hour we renounce a throne, and the pomp and power of the world, or cling to it. Hour by hour we achieve Nirvana in some immeasurable degree, and savour the sweets of it, or else renounce it, to teach the Way to it to all mankind. In the end we earn, else should we not receive, brief flashes of eternity, immortal moments whose gain is absolute and does not fade. Yet a description of them, if such be possible, is of little use to the pilgrim save as he proves it to be true upon the Way. 'When the pupil is ready the master appears.' Only the Master can tell the student that his new-found vision is genuine. Meanwhile the Way leads to Enlightenment. In due course the Light will more and more, and quite unmistakably, appear.

Our knowledge of Enlightenment must therefore be comparative. It is easier to begin with un-enlightenment, our present state of mind. Can we not see in our own minds, as in our neighbours', the ignorance, stupidity, darkness and sloth which screens the light of Enlightenment from their eyes and our own? The great minds that we know are luminous, serene, and wide of vision as those who view great distances. When this vision is raised in quality to the knowledge, direct and im-mediate, of cosmic happenings, shall we not strive to expand our earthbound intellects to something of their range of view? Lift the standard or plane of achievement further still, to the actual awareness of the One which lies beyond yet within the many, and the great ones of the earth are at your side. From such minds came the *Bhagavad Gita*, the *Voice of the Silence*, the *Tao Te Ching*. They know, but find all words inadequate. Yet knowing, they do not claim their reward, but patiently, for endless lives, attempt to expand, by precept and sweet reasoning, the countless narrow minds in which the fires of hatred, lust and illusion burn unceasingly. In them is a range of vision past imagining, a cool serenity which we can feel but not achieve, a sense of Oneness which is quite unshaken in the face of difference, a deep compassion for all living things which acts and does not waste its substance in mere words. These men are known to us, though not to the full range of their titanic minds. If these are more enlightened than ourselves, they surely serve as a model for our own development. What more they can attain they only know. We, too, shall know when we stand beside them. Meanwhile, between ourselves and their achievement is a long stretch of the Way. How shall we reach them unless we begin, with fierce and strenuous beginning, that long yet joyous journey and first, by developing a deep understanding of the principles on which it is planned?

CHAPTER TWO

THE BASIC PRINCIPLES OF BUDDHISM

So much for the human Buddha, his Enlightenment. What did he teach? It is not easy to know precisely, for like all Teachers he left no written record. But there is general agreement among scholars that the manifold Scriptures of the Theravada School, the 'Teaching of the Elders' found today in Ceylon, Burma, Thailand and Cambodia, contain a great deal of the basic teaching as given to his *Bhikkhus,* the monks of the Order or *Sangha* which he founded.

It is of profound importance that these basic principles should be thoroughly assimilated by those who aspire to Zen awareness. This applies, we believe, to students everywhere, but all the more to those of Western upbringing, where these basic facts of life are either completely unknown or at least glossed over in favour of doctrines which the Buddhist rejects as demonstrably untrue. Let us look, then, at some of the teachings of this oldest school of Buddhism, and let not the would-be student of Zen Buddhism for one moment despise them, or regard them as fit only for beginners in the field of spiritual awareness. This School, flourishing today, with a large Canon now fully translated into English and other tongues, has stood the wear and tear of twenty-five centuries. During that period, first transmitted by memory and in the first century B.C. written down, these Scriptures may have suffered omissions, additions and much 'editing' until, as one great scholar believed, the deeper truths pronounced by the Buddha were left but as nuggets of gold in a field of dross. This is an extreme view; the other is to regard the whole Canon, as the Fundamentalists regard the Bible, as totally inspired. Between these views the learner Buddhist must pick his middle way, in this as in all things, and he will find for himself a body of principles which comprise a practical, rational moral-philosophy sufficient for most men for this life and many to come. Here is philosophy, ethics and psychology presented in the scientific idiom of proven fact. Here is a textbook of mind control, analysis and development, and a way of life within a testable law of Cause-Effect which operates in every corner of life to give its user the power to make himself what he would be, even as his past thoughts and actions have made him what he is.

Let us then study these principles, for their digestion in the mind may prove essential in raising the level of consciousness to a point where doctrine, small and great, can be transcended in the awareness of No-Mind. They are often summarized as the three Signs of Being, the four Noble Truths, including the Middle Way of the Noble Eightfold Path, Karma and Rebirth, Concentration and Meditation, the absence of Authority in Buddhism and its consequent Tolerance, and something of Nirvana, already briefly described. Let us look at the Three Signs of Being.

The Three Signs of Being

These characteristics of existence, or qualities of all phenomena, are not doctrine but fact, and their existence should be tested by every student for himself before he accepts them. There is then time to test the inferences and appropriate action which the great Teacher advised as flowing from the fact. All aggregates, compounded things, compounds or formations, said the Buddha, will be found to be *anicca*, subject to change, and *dukkha,* inseparable from suffering in one form or another, and all things whatsoever, even though we call them elements and not compounds, will be found to be *anatta*, meaning devoid of a separate self. The distinction between elements and compounds is no longer of great importance to us, for even Western science now admits that the atom is infinitely complex, and that in the last analysis there is no such thing as matter, only movement or flow. All things, events, happenings, seen and unseen, existing visibly or only in the mind are, in Buddhist eyes, perpetually changing and impermanent, without any exception whatsoever; all things are equally *dukkha,* that is, incomplete, imperfect, 'joined to the unloved, separated from the loved', and all are equally *anatta,* without a separate soul or self which eternally marks them as distinct from other things.

The list is not fortuitous. If the Buddha emphasized these three it is because these three, and their intimate and complex interrelation, form a central position in his philosophy of life, which was in turn the product of his spiritual experience.

'All things are changing.' As a statement of fact this is trite. It is scientifically obvious, and as applied to human life, is the subject of perennial sermons, poems and sentimental regret. The cycle of form is everywhere apparent. All that we know, visible and invisible, of tangible fact or intangible concept, proves the cycle of birth, growth, decay and death, while the life which used the form moves on. Life is flow, movement. The law of progress, or regress, is a perpetual becoming; it is we who add the epithets of 'better' or 'worse' to the next stage in the process. *Karma,* the universal law of cause-effect, is rightly called the mode of change, for it is the law of cause-effect wherein the change develops as it does and not otherwise. Rebirth is the field of change in time.

To agree that all is in a state of flux is easy, but to use the law, to mould habitual thought and enterprise to accord with its cold decree, this is unusual, but worth the effort involved. 'Life is a bridge; walk over it, but build no house upon it.' What admirable advice, but what does it imply? It means that on this earth there is no such thing as security, and it is useless to look for it. It means that the wise man uses what Alan Watts has rightly called 'the wisdom of insecurity', and accepts the flow of life as he accepts the law of gravity. Happiness, indeed, begins when we live as if *anicca* were true. In a world of change there can be no 'authority', human or otherwise. All, without exception is changing. There is therefore no such thing as static ownership, for that which owns is changing rapidly, faster probably than that which it claims to own. Even possession is suspect. Do I truly possess some much-loved ornament? If so, what possesses it? My body, my emotions, my mind? All are changing, and soon the 'I' and the object will alike be very different. Regret for old age, and the passing of this and that is clearly foolish; so also is the longing for a state of things which has not yet arrived. There is a charming story of an Indian prince who sent for his jeweller and asked him to make a ring with a phrase engraved on it which would sustain him in adversity and abate his pride in moments of success. The jeweller made the ring, and on it the prince, delighted, read: 'It will pass.' The wise man sees the truth of Kipling's phrase, and when he meets with triumph or disaster 'treats these two impostors just the same'. The Wheel turns, and we on the edge of it resist the turning. Yet at the hub there is only Here, and Now, and This, and change makes no disturbance. At the heart of the tornado there is peace; at the heart of change there is peace, but it only comes to the man who accepts the law and uses it to his own fulfilment.

Dukkha is the converse of *sukha,* usually translated happiness. To equate it with the extremes of suffering or grief is to distort the teaching in order to evade its power. It has been argued that Buddhism is a philosophy of suffering. But if suffering, in the sense of a feeling of frustration, dissatisfaction, and the like is true, and capable of proof by any man, why should it not be emphasized? None can doubt the fact of *dukkha* and its omnipresence. At a given moment a man may claim to be 'happy', whatever that may mean, but is his neighbour happy next door? And if not, what is the quality of happiness that is indifferent to his neighbour's woe?

The recognition of suffering and its cause may be used for the mind's development. But the mind's attempts to escape from suffering are legion in number and infinite in form.

We shrink from the dentist and make more fuss about a sore finger than in our more dispassionate moments we would care to admit. We run from emotional pain. We will not read of that which hurts our pride or fears or 'feelings'. We forget, or gloss over, or excuse an experience which injured the tentacles of our personality. We forget the psychiatrist's definition of a neurosis as 'refused pain'. In the same way we escape from mental pain. We refuse to believe what we do not like. There are those who say that they do not believe in rebirth because they do not wish to be reborn. Do they equally reject the law of gravity when a tile from a roof falls on their head? We refuse to discuss what we hope is not true, forgetting that hope itself is a form of fear.

The wise man, therefore, accepts the fact of suffering, and its omnipresence and inevitability. He looks for its cause and considers the means for its removal. He finds the cause in self.

The third Sign of Being is *anatta,* which literally means that no 'compounded thing' has an *attā* (Sanskrit: ātman). The Buddha taught that in none of the constituents of the personality, the physical body, feelings, reactions, various mental attributes and discriminative consciousness is there a permanent element which distinguishes that man from any other. What is in common is not the property of any man, any more than the life which appears in each daisy in a field is the exclusive possession of that flower. There is life, and it functions or is expressed in infinitely various forms. 'You' and 'I' are two of them, but though you and I each have a 'Self', in the sense of a reincarnating bundle of attributes or composite character, we do not possess some 'spark of the Divine' or 'immortal soul' which is yours and not mine or mine and not yours, eternally.

So much for the doctrine that the self that we know is impermanent and, like all other forms, inseparable from suffering; that the nobler Self must learn to dominate, purify and control the self; that whatever self there be it is not yours or mine and is by the intellect unknowable. For the rest, as Dr.

Suzuki puts it, *anatta* is not a matter of doctrine but of experience. Yet the application of the doctrine is of the utmost value in the inner life, and probably distinguishes the Buddhist process of self-deliverance from all others.

So much for the Signs of Being. What is their relation? In the Pali Canon we find but little help. It is written, 'Material shape is impermanent. What is impermanent is *dukkha*. What is *dukkha* is not Self. What is not my Self that am not I.' Simple reasoning can expand this meagre hint. All things are *anicca*. All beings, and in particular mankind, are *dukkha*. The bridge which links the *anicca* of things to the *dukkha* of man is the latter's false belief in self, the illusion of separation. While in the illusion of *anatta, anicca* causes us *dukkha*. Remove the illusion and the link is broken. Thus *anatta* is the prime cause of suffering in that it is the base in which adheres the desire for self.

Again, all is *anicca,* and man is no exception to the rule. *Anatta* is therefore the application of *anicca* to man, in that all his parts, with no exception whatever, are without permanence and immortality. But man resents the application of *anicca* to self, and persists in the pleasant illusion that 'I' am important, that 'I', whatever my demerits now, will sooner or later achieve, earned or unearned, my ultimate salvation, to dwell thereafter in eternal bliss. Because most of our minds are dominated with self the thought of the end of self is horror, and the self fights valiantly to preserve its beloved illusion. This fight is the cause of *dukkha*, for when every unit of life is fighting for self-preservation, for self-aggrandizement, the reign of *dukkha* is established and for long assured.

Again, *anicca* is impermanence, the unreality of form. The implication is that life is One, and uses for its better expression a million million forms, including, but with no particular preference, the parts of men. In ignorance, the absence of light that fosters the error of self, we claim for self a separate existence. We act accordingly, and *dukkha* in a thousand forms is born and again reborn perpetually.

The Signs of Being, therefore, are not fortuitously chosen, and when the Buddha with his vast, omniscient mind, proclaimed that these were the signs or marks of sentient existence, it was not that these among others were worth the disciples' attention. Rather they form a complete philosophy of life, the premises of which are not delivered as dogma but as facts which each man must find to be true. Add to the Signs the Noble Truths, that the cause of suffering is the claims of self, and the Way by which that suffering may be removed, and only *karma* is needed, as the mode of change, to provide as much as any man may need for lives to come for his spiritual digestion.

The Four Noble Truths

Having established the nature of the three Signs of Being and their interrelation, we must consider further one which the West has seized upon as the symbol of Buddhism, the omnipresence of suffering. But this is true, as all who examine life impartially must agree. In the story of his own last life on earth we read of the Buddha's first sight of an old man, a sick man, and a dead man, and he marvelled that all the splendour and delight of life as he then knew it must sooner or later come to that end. Then and there he determined to find the cause of suffering, and how to eradicate that cause, for the sake of himself and all mankind. To this end he left his father's palace, and his wife and child, and went forth into the wilderness – alone. There he essayed all manner of austerities to win to a final understanding, but ever in vain. Finally he seated himself at the foot of what later became the Bodhi-tree, and vowed to 'break through' to Reality. On the full moon night of May, just over 2,500 years ago, he utterly succeeded. His consciousness was now commensurate with that of the universe; the illusion of a self was dead. In the light of omniscience which now was his he understood at last not only the omnipresence of suffering, but its cause. This cause, the second of the Noble Truths, he found to be desire, the craving for self which springs from the illusion of self; the lust for self-expansion and importance which perpetuates the illusion that the fragment of life with this name and address is in essence different from some fragment with another. This thirst or craving which feeds our self-awareness is the sole source of evil, for when it is dead there is no impulse to any act which works against the commonweal. Then what is the third Truth but the logical progression from the first two? If there is suffering and its cause is desire, to remove the suffering we must remove the desire. But how? The answer is the fourth and last Truth, the Middle Way, the eightfold Path to Nirvana which every man can begin to tread as soon as the suffering born of self becomes too great to be endured a moment longer. This is the heart of Buddhism as a Way of life, the slow, deliberate process of spiritual development through mental and moral purification in thought, word and deed. True, there are those who claim that all attempts at self-improvement only strengthen the self; experience gives them the lie where the motive itself is pure. Clearly, to work for the mind's expansion in order to improve the standing of the self among one's neighbours is folly; but until some measure of the wrong habits of thought and desire are purged from the personality, how shall it serve as the vehicle of achieved enlightenment? Again, it is true that morality is not of itself a passport to Zen experience, and may lead no inch towards it, but the light comes to a mind that is ready to receive it. Here, then is the fourth Truth, the Eightfold Path which has sufficed the Buddhists of the Theravada School for twenty-five centuries. Is there any better course of planned preparation for the rigours of the climb to Zen awareness?

The Middle Way is no mere compromise between the 'pairs of opposites'. It is not a middle way between good and evil, nor between too much effort and too little. The key to its nature is in the word translated 'right'. 'Right' Views, 'Right' Motive, 'Right' Action and the like mean these things at their purest and best. When an act is 'right', it is right in place, time, author, purpose and method of doing. It is done by the right person at the right time in the right place, for the right reason and in the right way. Hence the saying that there are two ways of doing everything, the right and the wrong way. So with each of the steps; each must be 'right' of its kind.

The Middle Way goes far beyond the field of ethics. Ethics, the right relations with one's fellow men, is an essential part of progress, but the ethically perfect man may be a long way still from Enlightenment. The Buddhist movement in England twenty-five years ago was such that the Buddhist was known by the fact that he was a vegetarian, and, if a woman wore no fur. Here is a principle sadly gone astray, a deviation from the Middle Path to Enlightenment. *Ahimsa*, the doctrine of 'no-harm', of doing no injury to any living thing, is excellent Buddhism. But it is far more important to think harmlessly than to create rules for harmless action; and it is more important still to think creatively and helpfully. The Buddhist about to enter the final Path will, as a matter of course, have achieved the control of sense, desire and thought which will make it unlikely for him to injure his fellow beings; but 'cease to do evil' is only the first of a threefold task. The second step is 'to learn to do good', and the third to 'cleanse your own heart', and thus develop awareness of the already-possessed Enlightenment. First clean the lamp by all means; then make way for the Light.

The Middle Way is not the life of the crank, still less of the egotist. Before one can be extraordinary one must learn to be extra-ordinary, to be as nothing in the eyes of the world. Personal ambition is a bar to spiritual progress, not a way to it, and the great men of the world have no desire for power in any of its worldly forms. The Way is a way of experience, and to the Buddhist all that happens is material for progress. We can learn something from everything, and 'there is nothing good or bad but thinking makes it so'.

CHAPTER THREE

KARMA AND REBIRTH

KARMA is the living law, perhaps the supreme law of the universe, which the seekers of Zen must use in the development of the total self towards its spiritual fulfilment. It operates on all planes, at all times, to all things and in all circumstances. He who studies the law and learns to use it wisely is only expanding the process of science which discovers and learns to apply the laws of the physical plane, such as gravity. But in truth it is science, with its awareness that action and reaction are equal and opposite, which is using a limited aspect of the total law which, as Karma, was known to man at the dawn of history.

The Sanskrit word *Karma* (Pali: *Kamma*) has three meanings. The basic meaning is action; thence action-reaction as an inseverable unit, and the law which governs their relation; and, thirdly, the results of action, in the sense of the net resultant of long series of acts by an individual or group. It is in this sense that Buddhists loosely speak of a man's 'good karma', or point to the 'evil karma' now being suffered by a group or nation for its collective action in days gone by. As such the law is profound and immensely difficult, and if we understood it to the full we should be masters of the universe. For the cosmos cannot be partly ruled by law and partly the child of chaos. Either cause and effect hold sway or they do not; there can be no exceptions, although the complexity of the interrelationship may be utterly beyond our present intellect to grasp. This law is indeed the key to all events in the world of time and space, and it is worth the courage needed to face what a full acceptance of it implies.

For if Karma is true it follows that luck, chance, coincidence and fate are words to be no more used. No man has luck, whether good or bad, and nothing occurs by chance. Coincidence is the 'falling together' of events by cause-effect, however obscure that sequence, and fate is a term for banked-up causes so near their discharge that no further cause can ward off the imminent effect. Such thoughts, applied to the daily round, are at first profoundly disturbing. I may meet a long-lost friend who is newly arrived from Australia. We meet in a street which I have not entered before, nor he. We greet one another, exchange a few words and part. Was this coincidence? The mathematical odds against it extend to a dozen noughts. Was it 'mere' coincidence? If not, have the powers of heaven and earth for a thousand years conspired to bring us face to face that morning at that place to say 'Hullo'? And what is luck but a label attached to the consequences of my own past action? And what is fate but those effects which now *must* happen? These thoughts must 'give us pause', but which is the nobler attitude of mind, to 'hope' that all will be well, yet to rail at destiny when things go wrong; or to accept the truth that all is happening because it must, that all that happens happens 'right', and all things do, in fact, work well? If the latter be true, then cause alone is ·of prime importance, and the emphasis of thought is changed from the sufferance of effects to the joy of a nobler causing. Henceforth the mind will live increasingly on the plane of causes, and learn to 'suffer', that is, to endure effects.

What is this law which so much of the world obeys and has used so widely for so long? Is it purely mechanical and blind? Or is it alive, as all the processes of thought, emotion, and our bodies are interrelated and alive? The Buddhist answer is clear, that there is nothing dead, that all the Universe is but the outward seeming of Mind-Only, and that every part of this 'becoming', by whatever name described, is indivisibly one, one life, one living law and one Enlightenment. This correlation of an infinite number of causes makes for an immense complexity of effects, and yet, as the stoic Emperor Marcus

Aurelius advised, 'Picture the universe as a living organism, controlling a single substance and a single soul, and note how all things react upon a single world sense, all act by a single impulse, and all co-operate towards all that comes to pass; and mark the contexture and concatenation of the web.' But if life is one, and time is a convenient illusion, it follows that the correlation of cause-effect is wider than mere sequence of events. Yet we see the relationship most clearly as a line of sequence, and so long as our lives are consciously moulded in the light of the one life, it matters not that we, the infinitesimal knots in the cosmic web, can only handle cause-effect, and further cause-effect, in moulding all things and ourselves just so much 'nearer to the heart's desire'.

If Karma is the law of laws, then love is the fulfilling of the law, and the awareness of the oneness of all life is the link between love and law. Truly we are members one of another, and 'it is an occult law that no man can rise superior to his individual failings without lifting, be it ever so little, the whole body of which he is an integral part. In the same way no one can sin, nor suffer the effects of sin, alone'.* In the light of this mystical and therefore super-intellectual truth, it is easy to see Karma as the law of equilibrium, and its working as the adjustment of a balance disturbed. If a pendulum is pressed away it will return with the force which pushed it, and to the place whence it was pushed away. He that disturbed the pendulum must suffer the effect until the force is neutralized in the acceptance, and harmony restored. Between man and man the law works out as love. 'Compassion is no attribute. It is the law of laws, eternal harmony, the fitness of all things, the law of Love eternal.'† And the precision with which the balance is restored is frightening to him who leaves his debts unpaid. 'Not in the sky, nor in the sea, nor in a cave in the mountains can a man escape from his evil deeds.'‡ And he is a fool to try.

---

* H. P. Blavatsky. *The Key to Theosophy*, p. 137.
† *The Voice of the Silence.*   ‡ The *Dhammapada, v.* 127

The perfect act has no result. Where there is no 'self' to push the pendulum there is no self to receive the return, and cause-effect is ended for that doer. When every act has become dispassionate, impersonal, and done because it is 'right', there is no motive in the act, good or ill, and the ultimate aim of 'purposelessness' is attained. Nor is this an impossible ideal. To use a homely analogy, when a man in front of you drops a glove and you pick it up and return it, did you act from a thought-out motive? Or did neither thought nor emotion enter your mind as you did what was obviously 'right', spontaneously? Yet if all living things so helped one another, without thought of self or hope of reward, in crises great and small, how large the difference to human life, how small the swing of the pendulum!

The law, then, can be used and freely used, and it cannot be 'interfered with'. All that we do is the result of our own past causes, for we are in fact the net resultant of our own past thought and action. It follows that all that we do, and all that is done to us, happens because it must so happen. The Good Samaritan was not 'interfering' with the karma of him he helped, while he that passed by suffered the grave loss of an opportunity. It is your karma that you should be helped, as you are, or left unaided as you may be, and it is your friend's good karma to have you as his friend. Away, then, with all thoughts of interference. Is the law of gravity disturbed when you hold an umbrella over your lady friend? Yet you have interfered, it would seem, with the sequence of drops of water and the spoiling of her new hat.

The avalanche which sweeps down the mountain cannot be stayed. Such karma is 'ripe' for reception, and no new cause of our devising can stay the conclusion of cause-effect. Such karma has the force of destiny, or fate. All else is changeable. There is an old, oft-quoted prayer. 'Grant us the courage to change those things which should be changed; grant us the patience to accept those things which cannot be changed. And above all grant us the wisdom to know the difference!' Most situations may be altered by the addition of some new cause, just as the movement of an object pushed by a dozen men may be altered in speed or direction by the strength of one more man. But even when a situation is too powerful to be changed, one's personal reaction to it is at all times capable of control. It may be that I cannot stop it raining but I can control, or should be able to control, my physical, emotional and mental reaction to the fact of rain.

Fate, then, in the sense of a force which we cannot affect and can only accept with patience and humility, is a doctrine only true for such karma as is over-ripe for change. Towards such fate we can but develop the courage to bear such ills as we have created for ourselves by previous action. Freewill and predestination, the delight of the school debating society, are not one of the 'pairs of opposites' but the same truth seen from opposing points of view. Our lives are to a large extent predestined by our own past actions, but the force which created these conditions is as free as ever to remould them or to modify them either at the causal or the receiving end.

But if all in the universe is karma-made, then so am I. It follows that I must accept myself for what I am before I can deliberately change it. Having made myself and all of myself it is useless to complain of the body I had from my parents, or of the sex or class or race to which that body belongs. Still less have I any right to complain to an outside cause for any lack of bodily beauty or health or skill; rather should I be ashamed of my own past folly that made me so. But if the garment of the mind, the personality, be self-created, so in a different way is the circumstance about it. True, it was not in this life that I made my body's environment, but it is by the Law that I am where I am. I chose, in the sense of creating magnetic links towards the whole of my environment, and all about me, body, parents, temperament and job are self-created and must be, if at all, self-changed.

The method of change is twofold, either by altering circumstance or by changing my reaction, physical and mental, towards it. The first is extrovert activity, and all men see it; the second lies in the mind. Thus the alleged antithesis of heredity versus environment is, like predestination and free-will, falsely imagined. I 'made', in the sense that I brought myself into, my parents' body; I made in the same way my initial environment. Thereafter I begin to change my body and all about me, and I change, by all I think and do, my reaction to that changing circumstance. I can, if I think it helpful, and most men do, complain of my heredity and present environment. It is pleasant to say, and believe, that 'if only' things were otherwise I could do such different things and be so different. But it is quite untrue. For those differences would only exist if I made them so, and if I made them so I should be different too. Complain then, if you will, of all about you, of the Government, of your employers, of your ailments, and your landlord, of your family, your lack of capital and your job. But as you chose or made them it would surely be more dignified to change them, if you will and can, and meanwhile to blame yourself for your creation. This is the practical doctrine of acceptance, to take things as they are because you made them so, and to blame yourself, without self-pity or untrue remorse, for everything about you of which you do not approve. Thereafter you may rise and, if you will, remould the universe.

Thus Karma is indeed the law of laws, and knows no compromise. Its work is to adjust effect to cause on every plane, whatever the size of the causing unit of life, whether man or group or nation. It does not reward or punish; it adjusts. We are punished *by* our sins, not *for* them. He who works with nature flows on the river of life to the everlasting sea; he who resists is broken miserably. But like all other laws of nature, Karma may be used. How? A man may take stock of himself as he would of his own business. What are his assets, and his liabilities? What is his output, and how could it be more? What stands in the way of his further expansion? What new powers are needed to that end? Having taken stock let him re-organize this highly personal concern. Much must be scrapped of habit and outmoded prejudice; much must be slowly replaced and new attainment acquired. A new spirit is needed, perhaps in the Chairman of the Board; stock that is seen to be worthless, of old beliefs and values, had best be destroyed.

But when the new broom is applied in action the office staff may prove to be difficult. Habits of mind, emotion and body have had their way too long to be lightly given notice; they may, indeed, make strenuous attempts to sack the boss! Creditors will press for payment; debtors seem unduly slow to pay. If Rome was not built in a day a totally new man, converted to a Way of which the end is self-Enlightenment will not be built by a mere resolution. But once the resolve is made there are but two rules to the opening of that Way; begin and walk on!

Rebirth

The doctrine of rebirth is a necessary corollary to that of Karma. If a man is responsible for the consequences of his thoughts and acts, he cannot escape the appropriate results by the death of his physical body. Even the suicide returns again and again to the situation he refused to face until he has accepted, in every sense of the term, the products of his own imagining.

Of the nature of that which is reborn, of the prevalence of the doctrine in the West and the problems which it solves, and of the avenues of thought flung open by this vast extension of the 'allotted span', little need here be said. Books have been written on the subject, and all may study them. But Buddhism, which stresses the futility of speculation, and trains the student's mind to the immediate task in hand, finds little profit in discussing matters which do not lead to the heart's enlightenment. Whether the bundle of attributes which is reborn be called a self, or soul, or character, it is, like all else in the universe, for ever changing, growing, and becoming something more. It is not an 'immortal soul' which, possessed by you, is different from that possessed by me. It is in fact the product of that which dies, and whatever the form may be, we are here and now, with every breath we draw, creating it.

The value of the doctrine to the Western mind is that it shatters the end-wall of our present life. Instead of a final judgement leading to heaven or hell, or a period of purgatory followed by eternal bliss, which equally offend the sense of justice and the heart's belief, the Buddhist offers a vista of an ever-rising path which climbs the mountain to a range of view beyond imagining. How long the path may be depends for any man on where he stands today and his speed of travel. These are his past and present choosing, but the beginning of the Way is here and now, and Karma and rebirth are the means of treading it.

CHAPTER FOUR

CONCENTRATION AND MEDITATION

THE habit, founded on the need, of mind development by meditation, is common to all schools of Buddhism, and a chapter on it might appear appropriately at any stage of this approach to Zen. Zen itself, it will be remembered, is derived from the Chinese Ch'an, which in turn derives from the Sanskrit Dhyana, a word which can be translated as meditation, and the Zen School is still widely known as the Meditation School of Chinese and Japanese Buddhism. Some basic principles of this universal practice may therefore well be given at this stage, to be elaborated as the need arises when we reach Zen Buddhism.

'Meditation,' says Dr. Evans-Wentz in his Foreword to Miss Lounsbery's *Buddhist Meditation*, 'is the royal highway to man's understanding of himself.' This magnificent statement is profoundly true. In the words of a Buddhist Scripture, 'Cease to do evil; learn to do good; cleanse your own heart. This is the Teaching of the Buddhas.' First comes the dual process of abandoning wrong ways of thought and action, and developing those which reflect the One and are therefore 'right'. But then there opens the true and final Path, the assault on illusion, the illusion of self and all its works, for the life of morality is only a preparation for the ultimate reunion of mind with Mind. The Buddhist goal is the full Enlightenment of the individual mind, a process wherein the light flows in as the man-made barriers of self are slowly cleared away. This process, as often pointed out, is not the salvation of a soul but the liberation of the self from self, of the individual mind from the illusion of separation. The process of self-liberation is therefore confined to the individual mind, though carried out for the ultimate benefit of all. It follows that no task is more important to the Buddhist; all else, the acquiring of knowledge, moral improvement, and even the practice of 'right action' are secondary, and in themselves of no complete avail. The reason is obvious, for in Buddhist teaching, 'All that we are is the result of what we have thought; it is founded on our thoughts, it is made up of our thoughts.'* In the cyclic process of becoming mind is paramount, for it is the thoughts begotten in the mind which manifest as action, 'good' or 'bad', according as the act moves towards Oneness or away from it; when the thought is right, right action follows.

The Buddhist Way, then, is a process of self-liberation of the individual mind, and the planned and unceasing work of mental purification and expansion fills the working day. The methods used have varied with the schools of thought developed in the vast field of Buddhism. In the West, the technique of the Theravada is well known, being set out in great detail in parts of the third section of the Pali Canon. It is widely practised today in this school of Buddhism, particularly in Burma, and great use is made of this method in the English branch of the Sangha in London. The argument runs: All men are suffering, and suffering from the fires of lust, hatred and illusion which burn in every mind. The fault is theirs, and arises from the illusion of self. As this illusion resides in the mind the mind must be purified by a strenuous course of training which will destroy the illusion, and produce instead the conscious awareness of Reality in which there is Mind-Only and no self. This process of mental liberation has two stages. The first is *Sati-patthana,* in which the mind is controlled, trained to see things as they are without emotion or thought of self, and prepared as a hand-wrought instrument for the final approach to Enlightenment. The second stage is to transcend the limitations of the instrument thus made. But only by mind can the mind be transcended, and there is no

* The *Dhammapada, v.* 1.

short-cut which avoids the early stages of the process; only through a controlled and well-developed mind can the final stage of No-Mind, which is All-Mind, be achieved. The spiritual insight so gained equates with the *Satori* of Zen, but the true relation between these and other exalted states of consciousness is a matter too advanced, and too debatable, to be considered here.

In the course of *Sati-patthana*, various advanced stages of consciousness are reached and transcended, and various supernormal powers are incidentally developed. All this is well set out in *The Heart of Buddhist Meditation* by the Ven. Nyanaponika Thera, but a teacher is essential for this strenuous course of training, and the student wishing to use it should apply for the assistance which he needs.

In the West, the need for some guidance in mind-development was made acute some thirty years ago by a sudden spate of books which were, whatever the motive of their authors, dangerous in the extreme. No word was said in them of the right motive for mind-development, the enlightenment of the meditator for the benefit of all mankind, and the reader was led to believe that it was quite legitimate to study and practise mindfulness, and the higher stages which ensue, for the benefit of business efficiency and the advancement of personal prestige. In these circumstances *Concentration amd Meditation*, a handbook written for the Western mind, was compiled and published by the Buddhist Society, with constant stress on the importance of a right motive, and ample warning of the dangers, from a headache to insanity, which lie in wait for those who trifle with the greatest force on earth, the human mind. At the same time Miss Lounsbery, of Les Amis du Bouddhisme in Paris, published her *Buddhist Meditation in the Southern School*, stressing the same advice to beginners. Both books emphasize the need of practice, as distinct from theory. Indeed I might here repeat the same two basic rules for a new practitioner, 'Begin, and continue!' In the practice of both rules the quality of inertia will strenuously resist the will. If it is hard to plan and to begin the long period of effort, it is far more difficult to continue, and only the early results, greater control of thought, serenity of mind and inner quietude persuade the beginner that the effects are worth the effort to produce the cause.

One of the earliest difficulties is the choice of English terms. *Samma Sati*, the seventh step on the Eightfold Path, is well translated as Right Mindfulness, but the eighth, *Samma* (or full) *Samadhi*, is often given as Right Concentration. In truth the term is untranslatable, but the three words used in *Concentration and Meditation* to describe the entire process are perhaps the most helpful and will here be used. Concentration is the creation of the instrument; meditation is the right use of it; contemplation transcends it. In the early stages, the first two should be kept separate, for different considerations apply; finally all are merged in the One-Mind.

Concentration begins with the practice of attention, full, impersonal, attention to the task or thing in hand. All successful business men acquire this faculty, for without it the day's work is impossible. It is in no way 'spiritual', being only the power of sustained and directed thought. It is harder to turn the same faculty within. A man who is proud of his ability to concentrate in the presence of distraction will be quite unable to turn the searchlight of his thought on to the nature and process of his thinking. The West is extravert, its power turned on the nature and use of external forces, whether of money, politics or the Niagara Falls. The older East is essentially introvert, its values being sought within, and the criterion of value being the mind's expansion in understanding as distinct from the worldly power of the personality. In either event the mind must be broken to harness and yoked to its owner's will, an immensely difficult task, as all who strive to focus thought on a chosen subject find. 'As a fletcher straightens his arrows, so the wise man straightens his unsteady mind, which is hard indeed to control.' From the choice of a subject which arises in the course of 'usual life', such as doing accounts, drafting an agreement or a complex piece of knitting, to a choice made for the sake of an exercise in self-control, is a large step, and the mind jibs at it. At first the subject may be external, a rose, a distant view, or the doorknob; then a subjective object will be taken. Breathing itself may be used, or the body as such, the emotions in their permutations, or the incredibly swift rise and fall of thoughts within the mind. Interest helps the power to concentrate; it is only at a later stage that the power is developed to concentrate by an effort of will on something without interest or, and this is of more value, to find interest in that which is, in all the circumstances, the next thing to be done.

Only when the mind is trained to obedience, as a small dog may be trained to come to heel when called (and to stay there), is the student in a fit state to begin to meditate. Immediately new rules apply; new aspects of the laws of life begin to operate. The would-be saviour of himself and all mankind is moving ahead of his fellow men. He is developing powers not known to, much less possessed by, those of his own intellectual standing. Just as magic is a knowledge of the laws of nature not yet possessed by 'scientists', much less by the common herd, so meditation quickly develops powers not yet possessed by the most efficient business man. Why, then, the teacher may ask the pupil, do you meditate, giving your time and thought and energy to mental development not yet achieved by most of your fellow men? It is vital that the answer be true and clear. There is one sole motive for self-advancement which is 'right', and it is not the aggrandizement of self. Indeed, as the inner development continues, the personality grows less, and with the withdrawal of energy from its worldly affairs may tend to fade out in the eyes of men. The sole motive for meditation is to purge the self of illusion, to develop the faculty of intuition to the point of Enlightenment, and to desire that Enlightenment, if it is desired at all, for the sake of the One-Mind. Anything less is evil, an abuse of powers, and the karma of such misuse is terrible. Think well, then, before you begin to meditate, and see that the reason for your vast new effort is 'right'.

For the first time physical habits become important. There are ample reasons for the right posture to be observed, for the time to be regular, and the place, if possible, the same. To strain is foolish, for the process must be slow, but if the practice is well conceived and regular, results will appear. Some of them will be unwelcome, and psychic visions and noises, emotional disturbances and alarming dreams may deter the would-be Arhat. The mental hindrances are worse. Miss Lounsbery mentions five: craving, ill-will, sloth, agitated states of mind and doubt. I have myself found many more. But the rewards are commensurate. There is quietude of body, as of emotions, and the dying down of the fires of lust and hatred which burn so tediously in the mind. Thought is steadied, strengthened and increasingly brought under control. The newly acquired impersonality of thinking, with thoughts bereft of emotion and of the constant reference to 'I', brings the clear light of a new serenity, and love acquires new meaning. It is compassion now which speaks, with the voice of the Silence, and provides the right because unselfish motive for every act.

This new affection for all fellow forms of life can be canalized in useful action. The four *Brahma Viharas,* for example, or God-like states of mind, can be usefully exercised at any time and place, from the office to a restaurant, from a dentist's waiting-room to a bus. These four virtues, though powers of the mind is a better term, are Metta, loving-kindness or good will, Karuna, compassion, Mudita, joy and Upekkha, equanimity or serenity of mind. In a famous quotation from a Buddhist Sutta, 'He lets his mind pervade one quarter of the world with thoughts of loving kindness, with thoughts of compassion, with thoughts of sympathetic joy, and with thoughts of equanimity; and so the second quarter, and so the third and the fourth. And thus the whole wide world, above, below, around and everywhere does he continue to pervade with heart of love, compassion, pity and equanimity, far-reaching, great beyond measure, free from the least trace of anger, or ill-will.' This practice is itself a subject of meditation, and as thoughts are things, and powerful things, and thought-force steadily directed is potentially an immense force for good, the practice of these ancient modes of blessing is a far better way of passing the idle moment of waiting, or a journey, than the useless and often harmful thoughts which otherwise occupy the mind.

The subjects of meditation are limitless. All virtues may be used, and noble thoughts, for as Epictetus, the Greek slave, said, 'You must know that it is no easy thing for a principle to become a man's own, unless each day he maintain it and hear it maintained, as well as work it out in life.' And how shall it be better maintained and applied than in constantly meditating upon it?

But it is always easier to keep up the pressure in a long and graded task like mind-development if there is a definite course prescribed. There are many such in Buddhism, and the student should decide his own. Thereafter what matters is persistence, and the due effects will follow the unremitting pressure of the cause. The hardest of all to practise is the joyous, inconsequent and almost nonsensical technique of Zen, which aims at no less than sudden, immediate, and direct Enlightenment, in flashes at first, but later as a fully developed faculty of the mind. It would seem, though the point is debatable, that Zen technique should begin when the mind has already reached a fairly advanced stage of 'right mindfulness'. Not until the intellect is well developed and controlled can it be transcended; yet until it is transcended, the Absolute of the One-Mind can never be known. To the extent that Zen has a specified ideal it shares the Bodhisattva doctrine of the Mahayana schools, for which see later, but the man who is dedicated to the service of all life, and in particular to his fellow human beings, must still perfect himself if he wishes to be of better service than a vague goodwill, and, as set out elsewhere in this volume, the Arhat and the Bodhisattva ideals are complementary as the two sides of a coin.

From Concentration to Meditation, from Meditation to Contemplation, such are the stages, and of the third stage little can usefully be said. At this level of consciousness, whether known as *Vipassana, Satori, Samadhi,* or by any other name, all words have little meaning. As is said in the *Lanka-vatara Sutra,* 'If you assert that there is such a thing as Noble Wisdom it no longer holds good, for anything of which something is asserted thereby partakes of the nature of being, and thus has the quality of birth. The very assertion, "All things are un-born", destroys the truthfulness of it.' For it is clear to the intellect that every statement is short of truth, for its opposite must, in the Absolute, be equally true. All pairs of opposites are relative, and only of value and meaning in a relative world. 'The Tao that can be expressed is not the eternal Tao', and descriptions of Nirvana, or the same experience by another name, are, as already pointed out, demonstrably untrue.

Contemplation, as defined in *Concentration and Meditation,* 'is an utterly impersonal awareness of the essence of the thing observed'. When self is purged from the mind of the observer, the trinity of seer, seen and the seeing is dissolved, and the seer sees by becoming the essence of the thing observed. The operative word is essence, as distinct from the inessential form. For the essence of all things alike is *tathata,* the 'suchness' of things, and this suchness is Void, (*sunya*) of all particulars. Only a mind in the void is No-Mind, resting in the state of no-thinking or Mu-shin, and only the mind that has reached such a stage for a second or an hour can know – and he cannot speak of it – the utter serenity and power that flows from Life itself into a mind that sets no barrier against it. But these are the fruits of mind-development. The tree must grow from an acorn to an oak before the fruit appears. First come the exercises, backed by right motive and an indomitable will;

then the right use of the new-won instrument. Only then comes the nakedness of a mind new cleansed of its own self-wrought illusion. This is freedom indeed; yet – asked by a pupil, 'Master, how shall I free my mind?' the Zen master replied, 'Who puts you under restraint?'

PART TWO

MAHAYANA BUDDHISM

CHAPTER FIVE

THE EXPANSION OF THE MAHAYANA

So much for the basic principles of Buddhism, as set out in the oldest, the Theravada School, now found in Ceylon, Burma, Thailand and Cambodia. We repeat, that until these truths have been deeply assimilated, only an exceptional mind can grasp the 'higher' truths of the later Mahayana, sometimes called the Northern School, of Tibet, Mongolia, China, Korea and Japan. Yet these expanded and deepened truths, and the Scriptures which enshrine them, are the everyday coinage of Zen stories, analogies, quotations and allusions, and represent the highest level which words can reach in describing for our benefit the indescribable.

How, then, have we 'reconditioned' our Western mind by assimilation of the basic principles of the earlier school?

We have learned to face facts, to some extent to see things as they are without attaching the labels of pleasant and unpleasant. This new seeing will be found to be the basis of Zen 'seeing', to be described later. But if all is indeed changing, much will have happened in our attitude to circumstance. It was Alan Watts who coined the invaluable phrase, 'the Wisdom of Insecurity' for his book of that title, and we must give up our longing for security for our belongings and our lives. We must accept the cycle of birth and death, and be willing to flow with events wherever they may lead us. We must then face the unpalatable fact, central to the Zen School as to all others of Buddhism, that what we call the self is no exception to this rule. All the components of the personality, the five Skandhas of body, feelings, perceptions, karmic impulses and consciousness, are found to contain no 'Self' which we can call our own, still less a SELF which is immortal and permanent. The thing we call 'I' is an illusion, and we have to change our whole outlook on life to accord with the new discovery. Then what is ours, which is permanently and immortally 'I'? Nothing, for THAT which alone is beyond change is no thing or principle that we can with the intellect cognize or know, still less is it in any sense ours. It may be that we are It; meanwhile the negative is all-important, that what we think we are we are not. Until this truth has well sunk in we can never face the tremendous principles of the Mahayana, ending with the Zen truth that there is no one who gains Enlightenment!

So to the third Sign of Being, suffering. This is a fact; let us face it. If any man is happy, or so he thinks at any moment, he lacks imagination, for his neighbour is not. And if his neighbour is sick, depressed, in want, shall he be happy? Then what is the cause of unhappiness? The four Noble Truths give answer, and the fourth is that Middle Way proclaimed by the Buddha in his first Sermon after his Enlightenment, a self-directed march to the Goal. The march and each step of it can be controlled by knowledge of the law of Karma: henceforth none can stop us in that march, although it is equally true that none can greatly help. 'Work out your own salvation with diligence,' said the Buddha, and the Buddhist strives to obey.

But this is an inward journey into the deeps of the human mind. The mind must therefore be examined, charted, known in its nature and workings. The individual must take the wheel of the ship of his becoming, and be responsible for all its movements. To this end he will learn to control and begin to develop the faculties he will need on the voyage. Hence the need of concentration, to control the machine of thinking, and meditation, to expand its range and power. But already there will be a dim awareness that all life is one, produced by a study of the doctrine of change and anattā, no-self. There will be a growing sense of no-separateness of the forms of life, of the spiritual solidarity of mankind and thence of every form of life. Somewhere here comes the birth of compassion, a nobler faculty of the mind than that which is called love, an impersonal, utterly spiritual power which is the expression of a corresponding development in Wisdom, and its immediate and perpetual expression. Not for nothing was the Buddha called the All-Compassionate One as well as the All-Enlightened One.

So far have we come; let us now look at the Schools which between them raised the whole level of Buddhism from that of an excellent but limited moral-philosophy to the widest, highest and noblest field of human spiritual achievement.

Just when and where, and even why this Mahayana School arose is of little importance to the Zen Buddhist. He is concerned with spiritual achievement now, with the nature and powers of the mind now, on the way to discovering the Here and Now and perpetual relation to This which will become his sole concern. Indeed the time may come when the distinction between the two main Schools of Buddhism and the relation between them will be of little interest to the Western Buddhist. Meanwhile it is necessary to know something of the differences, first in order to understand the current literature on Buddhism, which contains books on 'Buddhism' which blandly ignore the existence of the other school, and secondly to see them as two halves or parts of one whole, as necessary to each other as the male/female principle of mankind. It may be that this blurring of distinctions, and loss of interest in difference, may be a major contribution of the Western mind to the ever-changing field of Buddhism, for the West is eclectic in its inner life, and will choose without apology from this school and that of Buddhism just what it needs for its spiritual sustenance.

Here, then, it will suffice to say, as I said at some length in my Penguin *Buddhism,* that the distinctions are clearly complementary, that the limited range of the earlier school demanded the development, in those of opposite emphasis of mind, of those aspects of the religious and spiritual life which the other lacked. When we have looked at some of the principles developed in the Mahayana as the centuries went by it will be seen whether this thesis commends itself to others.

The general effect of the change, which began very shortly after the Buddha's passing, was to raise a moral philosophy of right action to a mystical idealism of spiritual becoming which engaged the total man. Emphasis shifted from the Arhat ideal of the 'worthy' one to that of the Bodhisattva, the master of compassion, as will be shown later. In the field of philosophy and psychology there was a lift from a somewhat materialistic view of cause-effect and the cycles of becoming to the supernal doctrines of Sunyatā, the Voidness or Emptiness of all things, and of Jijimuge, the Japanese term for the unimpeded inter-diffusion of all particulars', as Dr. Suzuki translates the term, achieved in the Kegon School of Japanese Buddhism. If these concepts are still in the realm of duality, and in the field of Samsara, everyday life, they are surely near to the break-through to Non-duality, an awareness of the Absolute. The intellect, as will be shown in greater detail later, can never grasp directly, and can only know *about* the subject of inquiry. When Jijimuge is grasped even at conceptual level the reach of concept is all but attained, and thought can go no further.

With the shift of emphasis to the heart, as guided by the intuition, from the intellect, ruled by the reason of the head, there is a broadening down of the Teaching to suit the needs of all men, and a consequent diminution in the prestige and symbolic value of the Bhikkhu or monk. There was therefore a profound change in the status of the Sangha, the Buddhist Order, and the monastery was no longer the centre of Buddhist life. This will be found to be of great importance when we come to consider life in a Zen monastery as distinct from the equivalent in the earlier school.

But the most profound change, and one of the earliest to develop is in the nature of Buddhahood. Let us consider it at greater length, for it is vital in Zen Buddhism.

Gautama Siddhartha, son of a princeling of the Sakya clan in North-East India, lived as man in the sixth century B.C., and his life can be pieced together from records which form part of the Scriptures of the Theravada School. But this brilliant mind in a beautiful body, who lived a life of symbolic perfection, was early associated with an esoteric, unwritten tradition of a line of Buddhas, Enlightened Ones, of whom Gautama Buddha was the fourth of his line. As such, these men were more than men; they were vehicles for a cosmic Principle of Buddhahood which from time to time would use the body of a man to teach the timeless Way to Enlightenment. This doctrine is not new, and is found in various corners of the field of comparative religion, the most famous example, perhaps, being that of Jesus who became the Christ. For just as Christos is a title and Jesus, when the instrument of such, was Jesus the Christos, the Anointed One, so Gautama became Buddha, the Enlightened One. But this inner Principle is innate in all mankind, else it could never appear. It follows that we are all, potentially, Buddha, and the process of self-enlightening is a process of becoming what we are, of knowing consciously our true nature, of becoming one with this Principle. Unless each human mind is a reflection of the Buddha-mind, of Mind-Only, how can the mind achieve reunion with the All-Mind? Hence an increasing realization of the truth proclaimed in *The Voice of the Silence*, itself a scripture of Tibetan Buddhism, 'Look within – thou *art* Buddha.' From a growing realization of this fact, that we are all enlightened all the time and only need to know it, comes the full development of compassion, the divine because universal force which is Wisdom in action. From this in turn flows the doctrine of *ahimsa*, non-hurting, harmlessness to every living thing because it, too, has the Buddha-nature within.

Finally, Buddhahood itself became a concept for the Reality which is supreme Enlightenment, being yet another attempt to name the Absolute. For if Buddhism is in one sense atheistic, knowing nothing of the concept of an Almighty

and yet personal God who created the universe, yet even in
the Scriptures of the Southern School there is a famous passage
which runs, 'There is an Unborn, a Not-become, a Not-made,
Not-compounded. If there were not this Unborn, this Not-
become, this Not-made, Not-compounded, there could not be
any escape from what is born, become, made and compounded.'* This is not God, in the Christian sense, but it is
the Buddhist equivalent. In terms of Zen it is what we are, it
is all that *is*. All else is illusion. From the human point of view
this Buddha is the Absolute, and so, from a prince who left his
father's palace to find the cause of suffering the Buddha
becomes the Supreme Principle, the God within, THAT which
manifests as the universe, which *is* the universe. Yet these
three aspects of the Buddha, the human, the Buddha within
and the Absolute Buddha are one, as man is one in all his
aspects. The search for Truth, or Buddhahood, or Zen, is
therefore a search for what we already have. We *are* Buddha,
in the sense of enlightened, already. All is Buddha, each blade
of grass; in Buddhist terms Samsara, the world of relativity,
is Nirvana, the infinite Beyond. In famous words of Dr.
Suzuki, 'there is nothing infinite apart from finite things'.

This change in Buddhahood is reflected in the change from
the Arhat to the Bodhisattva ideal. Indeed there was a time
in Buddhist history when the difference was so great that the
later or Mahayana School was actually known as the Bodhi-
sattva-yana, as if this change of emphasis expressed the scope
and purpose of what, geographically, came to be the Northern
School of Buddhism. Yet surely the actual difference is no
more than a complementary emphasis, as in the sex of humanity. If Professor Jung is right, our minds are so constructed
that in certain complementary powers and functions we must
needs be more of one than the other. Balance is an abstract
ideal, but the man who was truly and permanently balanced
would have to stay still, for the act of walking, and therefore
of walking on, is itself a rapid alternation between left and

* Item 1 in *The Wisdom of Buddhism*. Ed. Christmas Humphreys.

right, and all progress is in fact an increasing approach of the 'opposites'.

But each 'opposite' has its own opposite within it. Just as a man and woman have the organs of the other sex still present in a less developed form, so each of these ideals is only an extreme form of a type. Each has within it the dark side of the light, the vice of its virtue, the psychological shadow of its own unconscious equivalent. And it is this 'serpent coiled within the flower' of the virtue which attacks intolerantly the opposing point of view.

It is therefore more than an intellectual exercise to consider the two and to see how each in turn may be corrupted by its ever-tempting vice; to find out, each man for himself, his own ideal and why he pursues it, and to remember the right possessed by his neighbour to pursue the other. Only then will either see how in Zen a synthesis is achieved.

Who is the Arhat? In the earlier form of Buddhism he was a man made perfect, for he had purged himself of the Fetters, destroyed the Roots of evil, put out the three Fires of lust, hatred and illusion, attained the full range of spiritual powers and achieved Enlightenment. He had reached the fourth 'initiation'; having 'entered the stream' he had become a 'once-returner', and finally had achieved the state of an Arhat who, being self-liberated from the Wheel of Samsara, need never be reborn. He was, in brief, a man who had perfectly fulfilled his task, who has attained the Goal of Buddhism.

In all this there is, nevertheless, an inherent danger. The whole process is introverted. The emphasis is ever on the improvement of self. It is true that in Buddhist practice stress is laid on the elimination of this self, but whether the worker thinks of a Self to be purified and enlightened, or of a self to be destroyed, he is thinking of 'himself' in its manifold parts, and not of any other. And what is selfishness but over-regard by the individual concerned for the welfare and future of that which lies within his skin? The danger is actual, and was early seen. The Buddha's exhortation to his first disciples was to go forth and preach the Dhamma, to make it known 'for the welfare and benefit of all mankind'. Too soon, he seemed to realize, the would-be Arhats would become self-centered ascetics who, in concentrating on their own enlightenment, would tend to neglect their equal duty to make known to all men the wisdom which had come to them. In the result, the ordinary 'warm-hearted' laymen came to regard these cold, impersonal zealots as one-sided, lacking a sense of community with their fellow men. A movement arose to pay more attention to the needs of all men, to the exclusion, it might be, of one's own. From such a movement was the Bodhisattva doctrine born, to restore the balance of a Middle Way from which the zeal of the few had led them into the darkness of extremes.

What, then, is a Bodhisattva? He is one whose essence (*sattva*) is wisdom (*bodhi*), but the word gives little of its practical meaning. A Bodhisattva was the converse of the Arhat in that his prime purpose was to save mankind. He was extroverted to his fellows' needs, and his own were of no importance. He was the dedicated servant of all men, and so long as the least of them lacked enlightenment he vowed to refuse for himself that guerdon of a thousand lives. Later, the distinction was carried still further, and the older ideal was contrasted with that of Buddhahood, the Arhat remaining fixed at his own salvation, while the Buddha rose higher and higher in the celestial firmament.

Yet even in this flower the serpent lies concealed. It may seem nobler to speak and dream of a love for all mankind than to concentrate on the slaying of the self within. The danger of losing the Middle Way in the darkness of *Avidya* (ignorance) is quite as great. The Arhat-minded pilgrim argues thus: 'There is a cleansing to be done; the "I" must cease to do evil, learn to do good, and then cleanse its own heart So shall there be an end to selfishness, and thereby to the cause of suffering. Thereby the mind will be cleansed until all sense of self is ended, and it is filled with the light of Enlightenment. *What mind can I so cleanse, so enlighten, better than my own?'*

The argument is well-founded. As is written in the *Dhammapada*, 'You yourself must make the effort. (Even) Buddhas do but point the Way.' And again, 'Though one conquer a thousand times a thousand men in battle, he who conquers himself is the greatest warrior.' It is far easier to fill the heart with love for all mankind than to root out of one's own mind 'one fond offence'. The Bodhisattva ideal, in other words, may lead to laziness, to the replacing of hard work by woolly thinking, and the mind's control and enlightenment by a mere sentiment of vague goodwill. As Mark Twain truly pointed out, to be good is noble, but to teach others to be good is nobler, and less trouble!

Both ideals, then, have their purpose and their dangers, their use and their abuse. What is the value of the distinction to you and me? It is this, that all of us are more developed in one of each of the pairs of opposites in human faculty. We are more intellectual or emotional, turned inward or outward, concerned with our neighbours' or with our own affairs. The first step to the right use of our present talents is therefore to find out more about ouselves. What is our natural line of development? Is it a greater emphasis on self or on others, on inner or outward activity? The answer is for the individual, and the self-answer must be true. Am I running away from the task of self-improvement by interfering, though with the best intentions, in my neighbour's affairs, or am I spending too much time on self-development because I am little interested in the affairs and problems of mankind?

By now the truth of all this must be obvious. It is that neither ideal is better, the Arhat or the Bodhisattva, and neither alone is 'right'. How can a man achieve 'Enlightenment' who is indifferent to the needs of others? Can the right foot go on a journey and leave the left behind? Can the head achieve where the heart is ignorant, or the heart remain indifferent as the vision clears? Conversely, can the genuine and persistent worker for his fellow men fail to achieve the ennobling of all faculty, the heart's release from personal desire, the death of self, the increasing vision of the mind? In brief, we must all be Arhats, working diligently at the dull and tedious task of removing faults to make way for virtues, and steadily gaining control of a mind new purified. At the same time we must all be Bodhisattvas, steadily expanding the heart with true compassion, 'feeling with' those forms of life whose need is equal to our own. Both ideas are needed; neither alone is true.

The rise in the Bodhisattva ideal produced a corresponding emphasis on Karuna as distinct from Prajna, on Compassion, as wisdom in action, rather than on wisdom for itself. Yet here again the two are one. Wisdom is not wisdom until applied in one of the million *upaya*, devices, of the Bodhisattva mind which invents innumerable means of helping; and compassion, wisdom in action, is useless to the point of being dangerous unless it is the product of and guided by a corresponding wisdom.

With these universal forces, for they are no less, in full spate in a mind now partially set free from its hereditary 'conditioning', there is no limit to the range of thought save its own capacity. One result of this freedom is to sweep away the unnecessary analysis beloved of the Western scholar in which the functions of the mind are pigeon-holed into almost exclusive compartments. Students in our colleges and universities are encouraged to study philosophy, or religion, or psychology, or mysticism, or morality, as if these were exclusive factors in the human mind. They are not, and the very analysis creates some of the problems faced by the professors of each. Lily Abegg, in her *Mind of East Asia*, was one of the first to point out this fundamental difference between the approach of East and West to the mind. In the West it is piecemeal; in the East total, that is, with the whole mind looking at the functions of the total mind. A mixture of feeling, analogy, reason, and intuitive vision troubles the West by its imprecision and unscientific nature. Yet the East knows more of the total man than the West yet admits to exist, and the Eastern pupil/disciple at the feet of his master, under the ancient tree or in the modern class-room, learns more of his own mind and of All-Mind than the student of the West learns in the blinkers of analysis.

These considerations are a necessary foreword to some of the world's greatest literature known by the general title of the Prajna-paramita, literally 'the Wisdom which has gone beyond' (the limitations of thought). This vast collection of writings, ranging, according to Dr. Edward Conze, the present authority on the subject, from 100 B.C. to A.D. 300, is concerned with a number of themes which centre about the 'Void' and all that this ultimate concept implies. Behind all things is No-thing, which is not nothing; it is that which precedes all things and all thing-ness. Its essential nature cannot be described, but reams of great writing is none the less dedicated to the attempt. The most famous fragment from this mighty body of writing is the Heart Sutra, which is set out in full in the next chapter, and is recited daily in innumerable Zen monasteries in Japan. An equally famous extract is known in the West as the Diamond Sutra, of which various translations exist. Extracts from this are given in the same chapter, and the two works are set out with helpful commentary by Dr. Conze in his *Buddhist Wisdom Books*. But because these are doctrine 'descriptions about', however high the level of thought involved, they are only of importance to the Zen student to the extent that direct understanding of what they strive to describe is an aid to and in a sense amounts to Zen awareness. No attempt is made here, therefore, to describe the contents of these works, still less to comment upon them. They are to be studied, daily if possible, until the essential meaning begins to soak into the mind and act as a ferment for the intuition. The insistence on paradox as the only ultimate means for expressing Truth will during this study slowly acquire meaning, and the 'Suchness' of things, and the ultimate nothingness of all things, will slowly cease to be a playing with words and become clear statement of supernal fact.

Another pinnacle of Mahayana thought is to be found in the doctrine of Jijimuge, the 'unimpeded interdiffusion of all particulars', as taught in the Kegon School of Japanese Buddhism. For our knowledge of this we are largely indebted to Dr. D. T. Suzuki, whose description of it in a modern textbook I have not hesitated to use in *The Wisdom of Buddhism*, an anthology of Buddhist Scriptures of all schools, as itself a Buddhist 'scripture'. I attempted to summarize this teaching in my own *Zen Buddhism*, but here must summarize still further. At least this account will show the height attained by human thought, and the barrier beyond which reason cannot go. Thereafter only the intuition can announce, beyond all argument, 'I *know*'! Ji, then, are things, events, particulars, while Ri is the principle, the abstract, totality. Ji is discriminated; Ri is non-discrimination. Ri is the Void of the earlier scriptures above described; Ji is the ever-changing form, the things which are not to be found in the Void but whose essence is Suchness (*tathata*), which again is Ri. The supreme affirmation is, first that all Ji are Ri, which is not difficult to understand, for all particulars flow from their generalizations, and secondly, that all Ji are completely and utterly *each other*. Thus the parts of an orange are one with the orange, but, and this is the leap beyond reason, the parts are separately and together each other part. Spread this wider and it still holds. The apple may be one with the tree it has left; the doorknob is one with the door it is used to open; but the apple and the doorknob *are one*; all apples are all doorknobs, and each is the other. The brain reels, and argues that this is mere playing with concepts. So it is, until it becomes something more, but the layers or levels in the human mind do not of course exist in fact, and the analogy is apt to mislead. They are faculties of one ever-changing entity, and the intuition as it develops increasingly irradiates the field of thought. On its own plane it transcends thought, and by it we suddenly, entirely and absolutely *know,* but the purpose of Zen training is to develop this faculty, and in the process the higher ranges of thought are increasingly illumined by its light. Conceptual awareness is made brighter by this non-conceptual light, and the study of tremendous concepts brings the moment nearer when the subject and the mind that studies will, in a timeless flash, become one with the object of study, the thought or principle or thing.

Approached from what the West would call the psychological angle, this Voidness is an Unconscious of which the conscious mind, in the face of logic and mere sense, becomes increasingly aware, and Dr. Suzuki speaks of being consciously unconscious. The Yogacara School of Indian Buddhist thought produced the concept of Alaya-Vijnana, *Vijnana* meaning consciousness and *Alaya* abode, womb, store-house; hence a universal Store-Consciousness. This school of Mind-Only, admitting nothing to be true save the All-Mind which gave 'things' birth, is in a sense psychology at the level of metaphysics. Again, the development from the earlier school has been to raise the level of any principle to universal significance, no less, and the more material aspect is seen as a manifestation at human level of cosmic laws and principles.

To lift the mind from the lower to the higher plane is the purpose of advanced meditation, the complement to the analytic methods of the earlier school. The Theravadins, in the magnificent analysis of consciousness to be found in their Abhidhamma, the third division of the Pali Canon, reduced each moment of consciousness to its simplest elements, and showed the speed of change to be almost incalculable. The purpose of Mahayana meditation is the complementary opposite, first to still the movement to the level attained in Samadhi, one of a 'flat calm' of unruffled awareness, and then to expand this awareness until all sense of self is driven out and the mind moves towards All-Mind, finally to achieve, at first in flashes and then in great breadth, a consciousness of THAT which lies behind all differentiated consciousness, a merging with Mind-Only. But at present these are words and phrases, attractive it may be but of little value until they attain the validity of personal experience. Such meditation is for those who have learned to concentrate, in the sense of creating an instrument at the command of the will, and then have learned what for many is nearly as hard, to think in abstractions, to make cosmic principles and laws come true. Only then is the mind in a condition to make the return plunge, utterly necessary for Zen experience, when the abstract is abandoned, and Dr. Suzuki's words are found to be true, 'There is nothing infinite apart from finite things.' Then Sunyata, the Void, will be found in a flower, and the Suchness of things in the posting of a letter. But this is the goal, and we are far from it; indeed, we have scarcely set out on the journey. Meanwhile let us practise the mind expansion needed by a study of the supreme heights of human thought in words.

CHAPTER SIX

SOME SCRIPTURES OF THE MAHAYANA SCHOOL

As already indicated, these Scriptures treat of subjects which in a sense lie beyond description. They are therefore necessarily difficult, and full of paradox and what is to the reason sheer absurdity. It is not seriously claimed that they were written or even taught by Gautama the Buddha, although many are put into his mouth. Yet though the authors are unknown it is clear that they were men of great minds, attempting by every usage of language to describe for their readers what they themselves had found to be true. For scriptural writing, to be worthy of the name, must be the record, however inadequate, of personal experience; else is it no more than class-room lecturing. The men who wrote so firmly and clearly of the Void and Suchness and the triple Body of the Buddha-nature wrote of what they knew, but as the faculty by which they knew exceeds the bound of reason they could not make their writings 'rational' and within the rules of logic. It follows that the Western mind must exercise great patience, and be in a mood of humble but intense inquiry to gain increasingly the tremendous message which each writing is attempting to convey.

In most cases there are commentaries extant by lesser minds, each trying to assist still less enlightened minds to achieve the original writer's meaning, and in the case of two of the Scriptures chosen, the Heart Sutra and the Diamond Sutra, we have the advantage of a detailed commentary by Dr. Conze in his *Buddhist Wisdom Books* (1958). Here, however, the very minimum of notes are given, for the purpose of adding a chapter of the Scriptures at this point is partly to demonstrate the plane at which they are written, and so to rouse in the student an awareness of the faculty needed to receive their meaning, and hence the necessity of deliberately training that faculty as the search proceeds. This is the plane or level of consciousness which must be attainable at will for the study not only of these (comparatively) rational expositions of truth, but also of the Mondo (questions and answers) which are the recorded flashes of communication between disciples of Zen masters and the masters themselves.

The choice of examples might of course be bettered, and no two students would choose the same. But there is reason in the choice. The first few are from the great Prajna-paramita collection, treating mainly of the Void and Suchness; the remainder concern the nature of the Bodhisattva and his qualities. Read them many times and slowly; whole portions may with advantage be learnt by heart so that they may be studied at will at odd moments of the day. Do not, if a humble word of advice may be given, attempt to 'understand' them as one would approach a political argument or a description, say, of the Buddhist eightfold Path. Let the eye of intuition 'see' the meaning more and more as study deepens, for here is as much as words can say, and more, of THAT which we shall next look for in the field of Zen Buddhism.

THE HEART SUTRA

Homage to the Perfection of Wisdom, the lovely, the holy!

Avalokita, the holy Lord and Bodhisattva, was moving in the deep course of the wisdom which has gone beyond. He looked down from on high; he beheld but five heaps; and he saw that in their own being they were empty. Here, O Sariputra, form is emptiness and the very emptiness is form; emptiness does not differ from form, nor does form differ from emptiness; whatever is form, that is emptiness, whatever is emptiness that is form. The same is true of feelings, perceptions, impulses and consciousness. Here, O Sariputra, all dharmas are marked with emptiness, they are neither produced nor stopped, neither defiled nor immaculate, neither deficient nor complete. Therefore, O Sariputra, where there is emptiness there is neither form, nor feeling, nor perception, nor impulse, nor consciousness; no eye, or ear, or nose, or tongue, or body, or mind; no form, nor sound, nor smell, nor taste, nor touchable, nor object of mind; no sight organ-element, and so forth, until we come to: no mind consciousness element; there is no ignorance, nor extinction of ignorance, and so forth, until we come to, there is no decay and death, no extinction of decay and death; there is no suffering, nor origination, nor stopping, nor path; there is no cognition, no attainment and no non-attainment. Therefore, O Sariputra, owing to a Bodhisattva's indifference to any kind of personal attainment, and through his having relied on the perfection of wisdom, he dwells without thought-coverings. In the absence of thought-coverings he has not been made to tremble, he has overcome what can upset, in the end sustained by Nirvana. All those who appear as Buddhas in the three periods of time fully awake to the utmost, right and perfect enlightenment because they have relied on the perfection of wisdom. Therefore one should know the Prajnaparamita as the great spell, the spell of great knowledge, the utmost spell, the unequalled spell, allayer of all suffering, in truth – for what could go wrong? By the Prajnaparamita has this spell been delivered. It runs like this: Gone, gone, gone beyond, gone altogether beyond, O what an awakening, all hail!

DUALITY AND NON-DUALITY

Subhuti: How should a Bodhisattva be trained so as to understand that 'all dharmas are empty of marks of their own'?

The Lord: Form should be seen as empty of form, feeling as empty of feeling and so forth.

Subhuti: If everything is empty of itself, how does the Bodhisattva's coursing in perfect wisdom take place?

The Lord: A non-coursing is that coursing in perfect wisdom.

Subhuti: For what reason is it a non-coursing?

The Lord: Because one cannot apprehend perfect wisdom, nor a Bodhisattva, nor a coursing, nor him who has coursed, nor that by which he has coursed, nor that wherein he has coursed. The coursing in perfect wisdom is therefore a non-coursing, in which all these discoursings are not apprehended.

Subhuti: How, then, should a beginner course in perfect wisdom?

The Lord: From the first thought of enlightenment onwards a Bodhisattva should train himself in the conviction that all dharmas are baseless. While he practises the six perfections he should not take anything as a basis.

Subhuti: What makes for a basis, what for lack of basis?

The Lord: Where there is duality, there is a basis. Where there is non-duality there is lack of basis.

Subhuti: How do duality and non-duality come about?

The Lord: Where there is eye and forms, ear and sounds, etc., to: where there is mind and dharmas, where there is enlightenment and the enlightened, that is duality. Where there is no eye and forms, nor ear and sound, etc., to: no mind and dharma, no enlightenment and enlightened, that is non-duality.

From The Diamond Sutra

Section VII. – Great Ones, Perfect beyond Learning,
utter no Words of Teaching

Subhuti, what do you think? Has the Tathagata attained the Consummation of Incomparable Enlightenment? Has the Tathagata a teaching to enunciate?

Subhuti answered: As I understand Buddha's meaning there

is no formulation of truth called Consummation of Incomparable Enlightenment. Moreover, the Tathagata has no formulated teaching to enunciate. Wherefore? Because the Tathagata has said that truth is uncontainable and inexpressible. It neither *is* nor is it *not*.

Thus it is that this unformulated Principle is the foundation of the different systems of all the sages. .

Section XVII. – No One attains Transcendental Wisdom

At that time Subhuti addressed Buddha, saying: World-honoured One, if good men and good women seek the Consummation of Incomparable Enlightenment, by what criteria should they abide and how should they control their thoughts?

Buddha replied to Subhuti: Good men and good women seeking the Consummation of Incomparable Enlightenment must create this resolved attitude of mind: I must liberate all living beings, yet when all have been liberated, verily not any one is liberated. Wherefore? If a Bodhisattva cherishes the idea of an ego-entity, a personality, a being, or a separated individuality, he is consequently *not* a Bodhisattva, Subhuti. This is because in reality there is no formula which gives rise to the Consummation of Incomparable Enlightenment.

In case anyone says that the Tathagata attained the Consummation of Incomparable Enlightenment, I tell you truly, Subhuti, that there is no formula by which the Buddha attained it. Subhuti, the basis of Tathagata's attainment of the Consummation of Incomparable Enlightenment is wholly *beyond*; it is neither real nor unreal. Hence I say that the whole realm of formulations is not really such, therefore it is called 'Realm of formulations'.

Subhuti, it is the same concerning Bodhisattvas. If a Bodhisattva announces: I will liberate all living creatures, he is not rightly called a Bodhisattva. Wherefore? Because, Subhuti, there is really no such condition as that called Bodhisattvaship, because Buddha teaches that all things are devoid of selfhood, devoid of personality, devoid of entity, and devoid of separate individuality. Subhuti, if a Bodhisattva announces: I will set forth majestic Buddha-lands, one does not call him a Bodhisattva, because the Tathagata has declared that the setting forth of majestic Buddha-lands is not really such: 'a majestic setting forth' is just the name given to it.

Subhuti, Bodhisattvas who are wholly devoid of any conception of separate selfhood are truthfully called Bodhisattvas.

THE ZEN UNCONSCIOUS, SUCHNESS AND THE MIDDLE WAY

To see into the Unconscious is to understand self-nature; to understand self-nature is not to take hold of anything; not to take hold of anything is the Tathagata's Dhyana ... Self-Nature is from the first thoroughly pure, because Body is not to be taken hold of. To see it thus is to be on the same standing as the Tathagata, to be detached from all forms, to have all the vagaries of falsehood quieted, to equip oneself with merits of absolute stainlessness, to attain true emancipation.

The nature of Suchness is our original Mind, of which we are conscious; and yet there is neither the one who is conscious nor that of which there is a consciousness.

To go beyond the dualism of being and non-being, and again to love the track of the Middle Way – this is the Unconscious. The Unconscious means to be conscious of the absolutely one; to be conscious of the absolutely one means to have all-knowledge, which is Prajna. Prajna is the Tathagata-Dhyana.

THE BUDDHA-NATURE AND THE VOID

'What is the Void?' asked the Master of the Law Ch'ung-yuan. 'If you tell me that it exists, then you are surely implying that it is resistant and solid. If on the other hand you say that it is something that does not exist, in that case why go to it for help?' 'One talks of the Void,' replied Shen-hui, 'for the benefit of those who have not seen their own Buddha-natures. For those who have seen their own Buddha-natures the Void does not exist. It is this view about the Void that I call "going to it for help".'

SUCHNESS

Subhuti: What, then, is this supreme Enlightenment?

The Lord: It is Suchness. But Suchness neither grows nor diminishes. A Bodhisattva, who repeatedly and often dwells in mental activities connected with that Suchness, comes near to the supreme Enlightenment, and he does not lose those mental activities again. It is certain that there can be no growth or diminution of an entity which is beyond all words, and that therefore neither the Perfections, nor all dharmas can grow or diminish. It is thus that, when he dwells in mental activities of this kind, a Bodhisattva becomes one who is near to perfect Enlightenment.

THE BODHISATTVA'S NATURE

With mind unbending as the Earth with all her load; keen as the diamond in its resolution; unruffled as the heavens; uncomplaining as a good servant; yea, a very sweeper in his utter humility. With mind like a wagon, bearing heavy loads; like a ship unwearied in voyaging; like a good son beholding the face of his true friend, so, my Son, call thou thyself the patient, thy Friend call thou Physician; his precepts call thou medicine, and thy good deeds the putting of disease to flight. Call thyself Coward, thy Friend Hero, his words of counsel thine armoury, and thine own good deeds the routing of the foe.

The Bodhisattva's Training

The Lord: A Bodhisattva should not train in the same way in which persons belonging to the vehicle of the Disciples and Pratyeka-buddhas are trained. How then are the Disciples and Pratyeka-buddhas trained? They make up their minds that 'one single self we shall tame, one single self we shall pacify, one single self we shall lead to final Nirvana.' Thus they undertake exercises which are intended to bring about wholesome roots for the sake of taming themselves, pacifying themselves, leading themselves to Nirvana. A Bodhisattva should certainly not in such a way train himself. On the contrary, he should train himself thus: 'My own self I will place into Suchness, and, so that all the world might be helped, I will also place all beings into Suchness, and I will lead to Nirvana the whole immeasurable world of beings.' With that intention should a Bodhisattva undertake all the exercises which further the spiritual progress of the world. But he should not boast about them.

The Perfection of Giving

Sariputra: What is the worldly, and what is the supramundane perfection of giving?

Subhuti: The worldly perfection of giving consists in this: The Bodhisattva gives liberally to all those who ask, all the while leaning on something. It occurs to him: 'I give, that one receives, this is the gift. I renounce all my possessions without stint. I act as the Buddha commands. I practise the perfection of giving. I, having made this gift into the common property of all beings, dedicate it to supreme enlightenment, and that without apprehending anything. By means of this gift and its fruit, may all beings in this very life be at their ease, and may they one day enter Nirvana!' Tied by three ties he gives a gift. Which three? A perception of self, a perception of others, a perception of the gift.

The supramundane perfection of giving, on the other hand, consists in the threefold purity. What is the threefold purity? Here a Bodhisattva gives a gift, and he does not apprehend a self, a recipient, a gift; also no reward of his giving. He surrenders that gift to all beings, but he apprehends neither beings nor self. He dedicates that gift to supreme enlightenment, but he does not apprehend any enlightenment. This is called the supramundane perfection of giving.

From 'The Voice of the Silence'

Having become indifferent to objects of perception, the pupil must seek out the Rajah of the senses, the Thought-Producer, he who awakes illusion.

The Mind is the great Slayer of the Real. Let the Disciple slay the Slayer.

Saith the Great Law: 'In order to become the knower of ALL SELF thou hast first of Self to be the knower.' To reach the knowledge of that Self, thou hast to give up Self to Non-Self, Being to Non-Being, and then thou canst repose between the wings of the Great Bird. Aye, sweet is rest between the wings of that which is not born, nor dies, but is the AUM throughout eternal ages.

Give up thy life if thou wouldst live.

The Self of Matter and the SELF of Spirit can never meet. One of the twain must disappear; there is no place for both.

Thou canst not travel on the Path before thou hast become that Path itself.

*   *   *

Let thy Soul lend its ear to every cry of pain like as the lotus bares its heart to drink the morning sun.

Let not the fierce Sun dry one tear of pain before thyself hast wiped it from the sufferer's eye.

But let each burning tear drop on thy heart and there remain; nor ever brush it off, until the pain that caused it is removed.

These tears, O thou of heart most merciful, these are the streams that irrigate the fields of charity immortal. 'Tis on such soil that grows the midnight blossom of Buddha, more difficult to find, more rare to view, than is the flower of the Vogay tree. It is the seed of freedom from rebirth.

PART THREE

ZEN BUDDHISM

CHAPTER SEVEN

ZEN BUDDHISM

So much for the general principles of Buddhism, as formulated either by the Buddha himself or built up round his teaching by later minds. All the teaching so far described, and the Scriptures quoted, had their origin in India, but as the message spread it created for itself new forms and modes of expression which are loosely described as schools. As the teaching was taken towards all points of the compass, into countries of low or high development, these schools and their methods began to differ widely in their point of view and emphasis of doctrine. Thus the Buddhism of Japan and Tibet, and the schools within those countries, grew differently from each other and from the common tradition of the countries of the Theravada School. Yet the basic teachings were never lost, however modified, and it was not difficult to draft, as the Buddhist Society drafted in 1945, a list of Twelve Principles of Buddhism* held in common by all the schools in the vast field of Buddhism. One school, however, was from the first unique in purpose and method, the Ch'an School of China which became the Zen School of Japan. If the foundations of the building called Buddhism are best seen in the Theravada School, and the Mahayana schools may be viewed as so many rooms on the first floor, then the Zen School is the top storey, above which there are no more, nor any roof to the building which, at this level, is utterly open to the sky. Here, if at all, we shall find Zen and the Way to it, and the rules of the road. It is therefore worth while to study this great tradition carefully. In a later chapter we shall consider the vexed question of

* See *Buddhism*. Christmas Humphreys (Penguin), near the end of all editions.

'beat' and 'square' Zen, and to what extent the West must create its own approach to Zen outside the Japanese tradition. This is the problem formulated in my *Zen Comes West*, but not yet solved. For the moment, however, it is surely wise to learn as much as may be learnt about the forms of Zen which have served their purpose for fifteen hundred years, and led an untold number of seekers nearer, if not into the very heart of Zen.

Once again, we are not concerned with history save as it has a direct bearing on our training here and now. But the origin of the Ch'an School is important in that it illustrates the very qualities it now enshrines, a protest at the second-hand and therefore second-value approach to Truth of the existing schools, and its own new, and in a sense, unique insistence on a direct, im-mediate advance towards Reality. Let us then look at the state of affairs in China when Bodhidharma arrived from India in A.D. 520.

For the first five hundred years of Buddhism, the Theravada and Mahayana were developing side by side in India. Buddhism entered China in the first century A.D., but to the extent that it made any impression at all, it was not well received. The Chinese disliked monks who did not work for their living, but begged for their food, and even more disapproved of men who did not marry and therefore had no sons to honour their memory in the proper Confucian style. But as travellers brought from India the Scriptures of one school or another the Chinese scholars recognized them as great teaching, and were only too willing to study the new and exciting doctrines. By the sixth century, many of the Indian schools were established in China, adding a new factor to the existing tension between the shackles placed upon Chinese thought and behaviour by the tenets of Confucius, and the complementary freedom enjoined by Taoism.

Then suddenly came Bodhidharma, the son of a Raja in Conjeeveram, in south India. After forty years study under his teacher, Prajnatara, he became the twenty-eighth Patriarch of the Indian Dhyana School, and on the death of his teacher sailed for China, where he arrived at the court of the Emperor Wu in A.D. 520. We know very little of his life in China and less of his teaching, and what we read may be largely legend. But the effect of his coming is beyond question, and it was sufficient to change the whole course of Chinese Buddhism. According to tradition the interview went something like this:

The Emperor was a devout Buddhist, proud of his record of Buddhist good works. 'I have built many temples and monasteries,' he said. 'I have copied the Scriptures. I have converted laymen and made them into monks. Now, what is my merit?'

To which this silent, ferocious-looking Indian Buddhist replied, 'None whatever, your Majesty.'

The Emperor, taken aback, tried again. 'What is to be considered the First Principle of the Dharma?' he asked.

'Vast Emptiness, and nothing holy therein,' replied the Patriarch.

'Who then,' asked the Emperor, not unreasonably, 'now confronts me?'

'I do not know,' said Bodhidharma, and thus the interview ended. Thereafter the great man retired to a cave where he meditated for nine years and then quietly vanished.

But before he did so, he passed the Robe and the Bowl of the Patriarchate to a successor, who became the second Chinese Patriarch, Tamo, as the Chinese affectionately called the 'fierce barbarian' from India, being of course the first. A list exists of the Indian Patriarchs, from Mahakasyapa who received it from the Buddha himself, to Bodhidharma, though its value is difficult to assess. But the story of the first transmission is typically Zen and therefore worth recording. I quote from my own *Zen Buddhism*.

'It is said – and what is tradition but truth in the robes of poetry? – that once, when the Buddha was seated with his Bhikkhus on the Mount of Holy Vulture, a Brahma-Raja came to him, and, offering a golden flower, asked him to preach the Dharma. The Blessed One received the flower and, holding it aloft, gazed at it in perfect silence. After a while the Venerable Mahakasyapa smiled . . .'

But as Dr. Suzuki points out, 'This smile is not an ordinary one such as we often exchange on the plane of distinction; it came out of the deepest recesses of his nature, where he and Buddha and all the rest of the audience move and have their being. No words are needed when this is reached. A direct insight across the abyss of human understanding is indicated.'*

This was the secret which each of the Patriarchs transmitted to his successor, and the way in which Hui-k'o received it from Tamo is dramatic in the extreme. As the old man meditated, facing the wall, a would-be disciple came to him and asked for instruction. He was refused again and again. So he waited patiently outside the Master's cave, in the snow, for days and nights on end. Finally the will to achieve burst all restraint; he *had* to receive instruction. So he cut off his left arm with a sword and marched into the presence of the Master. Tamo asked what he wanted. 'I have no peace of mind,' said Hui-k'o. 'Please pacify my mind.'

'Bring out your mind before me,' said the Master, 'and I will pacify it.'

'But when I seek my own mind,' said Hui-k'o, 'I cannot find it.'

'There,' said Bodhidharma, 'I have pacified your mind.' Hui-k'o was enlightened.

From this story alone we learn three truths about Zen Buddhism. First, the need of tremendous strength of purpose before true instruction can be obtained, a demand for truth, it is said, as great as the need of a man whose head is held under water, for air. Secondly, the typically Zen im-mediate, direct down-to-earth attitude to a problem. Here there is no teaching, no explanation, and no argument. Nor is there any ritual or use of symbolism, analogy or invocation to any Third Party, or

* *The Essence of Buddhism.* Third Edition, p. 25.

God. Thirdly, this simple order, 'Show me your mind,' sufficed to give Hui-k'o that flash of Satori which is the goal of the first phase of Zen training. It was enough to rouse in him the deeps of mind, to show him his own enlightenment. Bodhidharma was speaking from his own No-Mind, and calling to the same in his disciple. In each was Buddhahood, and the Essence of Mind in the one called and had its answer. Our own philosopher, Bertrand Russell, has said that science is moving towards the proof that no thing is a thing. In pointing to Hui-k'o's Essence of Mind or No-Mind, Tamo showed him that Suchness which is in all things, including the thing we call the human mind. There is no thing; only the Suchness, which needs no pacifying for it *was* before peace and war were born.

These Question/Answers, which the Japanese call Mondo, provide the material for much of the Zen Scriptures, in the sense of writings which have appeared in the field of Zen. Collections of them have been made from early times. The earliest, the *Transmission of the Lamp* (*c*. A.D. 1000) is enormous; smaller collections are the *Blue Cliff Records* (Hekigan Roku), recently translated by Dr. Shaw, the *Gateless Gate* (Mumonkan) translated by Professor Sohaku Ogata, and the *Iron Flute*, translated by Nyogen Senzaki. Others which may be shortly appearing in English include the Rinzai Roku and the Sayings of Shen Hui. (For details of these see the Bibliography at the end of this work.) Succeeding Masters commented upon these cryptic Sayings, and others upon these comments, and the result is a mine of material for the student at any stage. Only the developing intuition will crack these nuts, and suddenly 'see' the point; but like a joke, the point is seen or not, for it is feeble when explained.

Already, then, we have several of the principles later codified in the Zen School of Buddhism; the fierce will to achieve it, the direct methods used by the master to help the pupil achieve it, and the Mondo, as one means of attempting to communicate the incommunicable. At some period an

attempt was made to formulate the Message of Bodhidharma.
Perhaps he did write it himself, but it matters not.

> 'A special transmission outside the Scriptures;
> No dependence upon words and letters;
> Direct pointing to the heart of man;
> Seeing into one's own nature.'

In brief, a direct transmission of the Wisdom without
depending on any outside aid, and direct seeing into one's
Essence of Mind which is Buddhahood.

This by-passing of the Scriptures was carried to great
lengths, perhaps too far, for study is a preliminary stage in
preparing the total man for the final assault on Reality. There
is the story of the master who burnt one of the wooden images
on the altar when he needed fuel for his stove, in order to show
his disciple that such lumps of wood were not to be relied on
as aids to enlightenment. And many a seeker, on finding what
he sought, went straight to his books and notes to burn them.
Yet some of these masters themselves produced great scriptures, and Hui-k'o's successor was one of them. He was
Seng-t'san, and he wrote the Hsin-hsin Ming, which can be
translated as 'Faith in the Mind' or 'Trust in the Heart', for the
word Hsin covers heart and mind in English. This lovely poem
(No. 111 in *The Wisdom of Buddhism*) is of the very essence of
Zen, and is interesting in showing strong Taoist influence.
I am not the first to call Zen the child of Bodhidharma and
Taoism, and much of Zen will be easier to understand after
study of the *Tao Tê Ching,* the brief and enigmatic classic of
the teachings of Lao-Tzu, a contemporary of the Buddha and
Confucius. The Indian attitude to the mind was domination,
to bring it under control, and the like with all behaviour and
thence as to nature herself. The Taoist attitude was the reverse
– to follow it, accept it, digest its will and purpose, and by
'action in inaction' to overcome obstacles which are in fact
but a product of the mind.

The fourth Patriarch was Tao-hsin who attained his own

liberation in a famous dialogue. He came to Seng-t'san and asked,

'What is the method of liberation?'
'Who binds you?' asked Seng-t'san.
'No one binds me,' said the pupil.
'Why then,' said the master, 'do you seek liberation?'

This was enough for Tao-hsin, who in that moment 'saw'.

The fifth Patriarch, Hung-jen, was, like his successor, a manual worker and no scholar, yet he is said to be the first great teacher to have a large following. Certainly about this date, A.D. 700, there was a great flowering of Zen, and with Hui-neng, the sixth Patriarch (637–713), we have the true founding of the Chinese Ch'an School which later became the Zen School of Japan. Hung-jen's two most famous disciples, Shen-hsiu and Hui-neng, epitomized the divergent tendencies in the new school of Buddhism, and from this classic divergence stems the distinction in emphasis in the two Zen schools, Rinzai and Soto, of today.

With Hui-neng (in southern dialect Wei-lang, and in Japan known as Eno or Yeno), we begin the Zen movement as such. If the long list of twenty-eight Indian Patriarchs crystallized in Bodhi-dharma, who became the first of China, so the two hundred years of Chinese Patriarchs, from about A.D. 500–700 crystallized in the sixth and last, Hui-neng. Dr. Suzuki has called Zen Buddhism China's reaction to Indian Buddhism, and others have added that in the same way Zen Buddhism is Japan's reaction to the Chinese Ch'an. Certainly Hui-neng was himself the epitome of the past and founder of the future of the school. There were no more Patriarchs, but a long series of great masters from A.D. 700–900 who between them consolidated the purpose of the school and its unique methods of teaching. But as we look back we see signs of a slow decline. There is more reliance on recorded Sayings as the subject for study, and less of the dynamic spontaneity which marks the great masters of Zen. But if the use of recorded Mondo, and the new device of the Koan betrayed a lowering standard of spiritual attainment in those who taught, it may well be that the carefully transmitted methods served to preserve the school as such, and to offer it alive and strongly kicking with spiritual virility today.

There is no room here for the life of Hui-neng, still less for a disquisition on his teaching. The former may be read in the *Sutra of Hui-neng*, translated by Wong Mou-lam, and the latter in Dr. Suzuki's *Zen Doctrine of No-Mind*. But it is important to consider the distinction between the two disciples of the fifth Patriarch, Shen-hsiu and Hui-neng, for these differences exist in our own minds, and we must choose. Shen-hsiu taught that Buddhahood is enlightenment, which exists in each mind, and can be seen if the mind remains entirely undisturbed. If undisturbed, the mind, which is now the Buddha-Mind, can use the senses and the functions of daily life while living in enlightenment. The mind is thus a mirror, and the dust of passion must not be allowed to obscure it. When, therefore, the fifth Patriarch was seeking a successor, and asked those in his monastery to write a stave of verse or *gatha* to show their enlightenment, Shen-hsiu, the 'hot favourite' for the Patriarchate, wrote:

> 'This body is the Bodhi-tree;
> The mind is like a mirror bright.
> Take heed to keep it always clean,
> And let no dust alight.'

Hui-neng would have none of it. He was merely a pounder of rice at the time, having little scholarship, but he had had his enlightenment years before on hearing a single verse of the Diamond Sutra, and he knew that he could improve on the favourite. So he got a friend to write for him on the wall where his rival's verse was written:

> 'There is no Bodhi-tree,
> No stand of mirror bright.
> Since all is void,
> Where can the dust alight?'

That is Zen, and in a sense the whole of Zen, whereas the dust-wiping school of Shen-hsiu represents but the quietest method of still meditation, Dhyana, which is why the Zen School is still called by many the Meditation School of Buddhism. Eno's shout to the world was nothing less than this, 'From the first not a thing is,' and his voice still echoes in the Rinzai or 'Sudden' School of Zen. To wipe at the dust implies duality, that is to say, dust and the Mind which is No-Mind. For Hui-neng nothing is, nor dust nor Mind, and there is nothing to be 'done' by anyone. (Cp. the Taoist Wu-wei, or 'action in inaction'). For him there is no How in life, nor What nor When nor Why. There is – the rest is silence, and a finger pointing to the Way. That is what Dr. Suzuki calls 'dynamic demonstration', and it ranges from utter silence to anything, a gesture or cough, or a blow, which will fully rouse the waking awareness of the agonized disciple.

Hui-neng's gatha, which secured him the Patriarchate, is difficult, for it is absolute and leaves no foothold for reason. It is not meant to, for all religious experience is in the last analysis beyond reason, beyond the duality of thought and therefore beyond description. From this standpoint all doctrine, and hence all scripture, is gravely limited, for it moves on the tram-lines of thought and never leaves the ground. The experience it contains is second-hand and therefore of second value. Hui-neng's teaching could appeal to the masses of little learning; he appealed to the intuition which is not confined to those of erudition.

Later, it is true, we must learn to balance even the two gathas of Shen-hsiu and Hui-neng. As Dr. Suzuki's own master, Soyen Shaku, wrote, 'they are the wings of a bird, the two wheels of a cart or, perhaps more exactly, one is like the eye and the other the legs' – and both are needed. In an absolute awareness we *know*; but it is in the world of particulars that we must act, and our training must be planned accordingly.

We must continue our history, and for the moment it must

suffice to mention certain doctrines which, by the time of Eno's passing, had become the stock in hand of Zen. First, the Unconscious of Indian philosophy had become Hui-neng's 'Essence of Mind' which is No-Mind. From a psychological postulate this Absolute had moved into the realm of mystical metaphysics made known by experience. Secondly, just 'sitting' in meditation was not good enough. Dhyana, meditation, must be wedded to Prajna, Wisdom acquired by intuition, which in turn was expressed in compassion. This distinction is of profound importance (and will be developed later). Thirdly, there is a new meaning in Zen 'seeing', a direct vision into things as they are, into their 'suchness'; and as this suchness is again the Essence of Mind there is an end to all distinction between particulars. Hence Hui-neng's famous 'All distinctions are falsely imagined'. Fourthly, Zen must be found, as he found it, in everyday life, not merely in monastic calm; and fifthly, the achievement of No-Mind is 'sudden'.

These new and profoundly disturbing principles were wide open to abuse, and those responsible knew it. If no thing is; if the mind within is the sole criterion for action; if nothing matters very much and most things not at all, why then be moral, self-controlled and 'mindful and self-possessed'? The Scriptures at least keep the mind and heart in orderly restraint, and prevent false teachers leading the still more blind astray; and the danger of the Zen form of release was treated seriously. From freedom from external restraint the heart must find the new freedom of internal discipline. Where No-Mind is truly sought, the mind and the senses can be, and must be, reasonably restrained.

From two of Hui-neng's disciples stem the present schools of Rinzai (Sudden) and Soto (Gradual) Zen. Shen-hui was a great master and his Sayings have only recently been made known in English for the first time. But it was from Seigen Gyoshi that derives the line of Sekito, Tokusan and Ganto and so to Dogen, the virtual founder of Soto Zen. From

Nangaku came Nansen, Hyakujo, Joshu, Gutei and, more important historically, Obaku (in Chinese Huang-Po) and Rinzai himself, the founder of the Rinzai sect of Japan. We must look at these two schools carefully, for the West may choose between them; at the moment it is enough to describe the Soto sect as the more receptive, quietist and feminine in approach to Reality, and the Rinzai as the immensely positive and fiercely direct way to the common goal.

The line of spiritual succession of the great Ch'an masters is excellently set out in the charts at the end of *The Development of Chinese Zen*.* Each of these men added something to the Zen tradition, and their collected and recorded Sayings or Mondo provide unlimited material for both the beginner and the advanced student in the field of Zen. For these Sayings cannot be understood like the great pronouncements of orthodox Scripture. The price of understanding is no less than victory in the battle at the other side of which lies Zen, awareness at a level beyond thought.

There were two great flowerings of Zen genius, the first in the two hundred years after Hui-neng and the second in the Sung Dynasty of China, covering, say, A.D. 900–1200. In the later period all the earlier sects and sub-sects had disappeared save those which survive today, the Rinzai (Chin. Lin-chi) and Soto (Chin. Ts'ao Tung). And as we are about to pass to Japan, this might be a convenient place in which to warn the reader of the confusion between Chinese and Japanese renderings of the same name which is inevitable where two peoples, with different languages, share a common writing. A Chinese and Japanese, looking at a group of ideographs, will 'read' them quite differently, and the student must learn the two forms of the name. Rinzai, for example, is the Japanese form of Lin-chi; the Obaku sect of Japanese Zen, now all but merged in Rinzai, is called after the famous Ch'an Master Huang-po; and Hui-neng himself is known in

* Dumoulin. Trans. Ruth Sasaki. The First Zen Institute of America, 1953.

Japan as Eno (old-fashioned spelling, Yeno). Conversely, when we read of Chinese masters such as Shen-hui (Jap. Jinne) and the collection of Sayings known as the Pi-yen Lu (Jap. Hekigan Roku, the Blue Cliff Records), we must learn to recognize the other form.

Rinzai Zen was brought to Japan in 1191 by the Japanese monk Eisai, who established monasteries in Kyoto under imperial patronage, and at Kamakura, the seat of the Shoguns, who were already ruling the country. The Soto School was introduced by Dogen a few years later in the mountains, in Eiheiji, for he was not interested in imperial favour. He was, however, an outstanding genius, and with Hakuin (1685–1768) is in the top flight of Zen masters produced in Japan. At present we know too little about Soto Zen, or of its Scriptures, which are in fact the writings of Dogen, but from what we learn in Prof. Masunaga's *The Soto Approach to Zen* it is clear that we need to know more before the West can have a balanced view of the Zen Buddhism of Japan.

The tradition has not died out, and both in China and Japan there are masters comparable with many of the great names of the past. The Venerable Hsu Yün of China, who died recently at the age of 119, was regarded as an extremely advanced teacher, and who shall judge the standing of those in Japan today who preserve the tradition and the Ways? It is enough that the Ways are open, and that there is still unseen, unheard, but not unknown, a transmission of Zen.

CHAPTER EIGHT

BEYOND THINKING

ZEN functions in non-duality. The process of thought, of reasoning, takes place in the field of duality. It follows that no thinking will achieve Zen. This proposition is fundamental to all Zen training, but the Western mind stubbornly resists it. So proud is the West of its highly developed function of thought that it is unwilling to believe that there is any knot that it cannot unravel, any nut that it cannot crack, even the famous Zen Koan. But until this illusion is dissolved, until the student deeply and fully understands that Zen lies, in its very nature, beyond all thinking or other mental process in duality, no progress will be made towards a Zen awareness. Thought can go a very long way; we can by reason achieve the concept of the ONE, the greater concept of the Void, the intellectual awareness that Jijimuge, the 'unimpeded interdiffusion of all particulars', must be true. But we are still reasoning *about*; we do not *know*. All systems of thought are content with ONE as the final goal of thinking; only Zen has the courage to discard this concept with all others. The opposite of ONE is MANY; Truth has no opposite. The Many and the One are but poles in a bi-polar field. Beyond both is Non-duality, which is not One, not Two, nor both nor neither.

Reason has built a palace of thought to explain the birth of the universe in terms of concept. From THAT came One, from One came Two, then Three, and thence what the Chinese call the 10,000 things. But we are still in duality. Let those who do not utterly appreciate this fact read further, for this understanding is essential to Zen training, and is indeed its basic postulate.

A good test is our means of communication. Apart from

gesture with an agreed meaning we have to use words. Words are sounds or marks of agreed meaning in terms of ideas or thoughts or feelings. They are symbols. When, therefore, we wish to transmit to another some spiritual experience, we must descend to the level of thought and wrap our discovery in the opaque material of thought and feeling in order to hand it to our friend. The friend must unwrap the symbol and extract for his own understanding whatever is left of the actual experience. This three-legged process must be repeated for the reply. 'How can I describe it?' we say to a friend of a sunset or a ballet or a book just read. How *can* I, save by this clumsy process of transmitted symbol? Will any symbol suffice to transmit the experience of being in love, or the fear of imminent death, or Satori?

The unit of communication is the concept, or thought, wrapped up in agreed symbols. As such it is second-hand, and dead, as a bucket of river-water is dead in relation to the flow that is the river. These concepts are the bricks of thought, with which we build a hovel or palace of thought, in speech or novel or play. They are made of the substance of thought in a form which has meaning to those who know that language and to no others. Yet these thoughts are things, containing a greater or less degree of life. A curse pronounced with full venom of hate behind it is a powerful weapon, as powerful on its own plane as a javelin on the body; the same curse may be no more than a conventional expression of mild annoyance. In the same way a blessing may be a mouthful of words, or a force for good directed with great knowledge. Thoughts are indeed things, but powerful by the force which they encapsule. Only to this extent have they any power; for the rest Jung was right when he greatly said that 'no concept is a carrier of life'. Only the human mind carries and can communicate life-force; in thoughts this power is for the most part locked up, useless, and being unused, dead.

Yet we create new thoughts every moment that we give an idea or feeling expression, in our own minds or aloud. 'It is raining,' I say, looking out of the window, and showing my annoyance; and you receive the thought /feeling, and react as you will, with further thought or feeling, or none. In the same way my views on Buddhism, or the new book I plan to write, or my belief in rebirth, all these are concepts, thoughts, which come from me and go to others, by word or deed. We are each surrounded by thoughts like a mass of barnacles. Old ideas, beliefs, intentions, plans; principles, moral rules, ambitions, even ideals. What a burden and how hard they cling! How hard they are to break, with forty years of solidification, it may be, from the stage of tentative hypotheses, mere gossamer threads of reasoning, to the concrete 'conclusions' (the word means shutting up) which only a mental earthquake will ever open again.

Even God is a thought, a concept in the mind; and some say no more, being a projection of the mind which, conceiving the thought from the spirit's necessity, flings it into the sky and then worships it. The Buddhist would call this waste of time, for God is real, by this name or that, but is only real as He or It is the Essence of Mind in your mind and mine, being All-Mind, which is Suchness, Void and Absolute.

Yet we cannot laugh at all the thoughts we create; men die for 'my country', fight for their 'rights', all but worship 'the State', and adore the Flag or the Throne. In the name of Liberty what horrors men will do, what murders and what nonsense in the name of Peace. But what splendour of self-sacrifice is found in the hell of war, what self-surrender in the days of peace, in the name of duty and love, or with no name at all. Yet remove the meaning from these terms and phrases, and how hollow is what is left. Only an empty palace, an abandoned shrine, the site of a battlefield of long ago. Are not our lives filled with memories of something we foolishly call I? They are all dead now, these things we once made alive and great and holy with the power of our imagining. Yet these concepts, weed-grown paths of thinking, dead ideals and wrong because untrue values, these are the obstacles which stand between our new-found striving and Zen. When the pupil asked, 'Master, what can I do to be free?', the Master replied, 'Who puts you under restraint?'

By the fetters of thought we are bound in a world of the 'opposites', and so far as mind is concerned we 'know' nothing save by a compound choice between them. If, for example, I want to describe to you my house I say it is old, brick-built, semi-detached, three storey and in London. By this you realize that it is not a new, concrete, detached bungalow in the country. All description of things, visible or invisible, is achieved by a build-up of selected terms chosen from a million pairs of opposites. Our thoughts and acts are themselves governed by this selection, and in driving a car we move on a middle way between opposites of time and space of great subtlety. We ceaselessly compare, in terms of the intellect, as to the more or less true; in terms of emotion, as to like or dislike. Of nearly everything we are clear that it is either this or that; it cannot be at the same time black and white, positive and negative, new and old, true and false. As the mind develops it accepts the possibility of relative truth, of a thing being this *and* that according as it is viewed from this or that point of view; we achieve relative perception and the perception of relativity. We are still in the dual field of the opposites, and we still do not *know*; we only know *about*, though it may be a very great deal about it.

As thought moves higher, and verges on the still higher field of intuitive awareness, paradox is boldly used to describe what a choice of the opposites cannot make clear. 'Give up thy life if thou wouldst live' is paradox, and the Heart Sutra is built on it. Now the other opposite is seen as present in each; male and female are seen as relative emphasis, no more. No statement is quite true, for its opposite is at least partially true, and one day may be seen to be equally true. This stage is of immense importance, for we must one day learn in meditation to hold the mind in enormous concentration of purpose, yet utterly relaxed; to seek intensely, knowing that the effort itself bars us from success; to see that the littlest act is of vital importance yet what we do is of no importance at all.

But paradox worries the intellect; it is untidy, inaccurate and useless in the field of reasoning. What, then, is the intellect? It is a machine, and though potentially a very wonderful machine, no more. It is dual in function, one aspect of it working at concrete level and the higher in the abstract field. In both it is a machine and no more. In the lower it analyses, discriminates, compares. It acquires knowledge about things and concepts, and can build them into plans for execution. It is the intelligence of daily life, in business of all kinds and social intercourse. It is always second-hand; its material derives from the senses, emotions and other thoughts. It creates nothing save further concepts.

Abstract thought is concerned with abstract ideas, generalizations, ideals; with synthesis rather than analysis, relationships rather than differences. It acquires knowledge about things at a higher level, but still about them; it does not know.

The intellect should be as a search-light, a precision instrument of great power under perfect control, lighting a chosen field of perception at will, and then being switched off equally at will. It is gravely interfered with by the least admixture of emotion. Like and dislike, hope and fear are out of place in thinking, whether for household accounts or the heights of philosophy. But the point here made yet again is that from the lowest to the highest level the intellect is an instrument only, using the material fed to it; *it cannot know*.

What, then, knows? Let us pass into the mind itself. It is full of duality. Reason fights with the senses, with the emotions, and blindly sets itself against the down-pouring light of the intuition. Consciousness is bogged in confusion between the subject and object. What looks at what? What is subject which looks at things, including its own mind? What is object that is not already in a higher sense within the mind? Much is written on this, in terms of metaphysics, psychology and epistemology, the science of knowledge. Here we can afford to pass on, noting, however, that until consciousness is merged with its object there are still two things, and we are still in the field of duality.

We have now reached a point where it is clear that the Zen we seek is not to be found by the intellect, still less in the field of thought. It is beyond, behind, above, the world of duality, however we view it. It is the Prajna-paramita, 'the Wisdom which has gone beyond'. But it is not the ONE, for it lies beyond the final pair of the MANY/ONE. However high we climb with the two feet of the opposites we must finally end thinking, and do something else. When we reach the top of the 100 foot pole, in Zen terminology, we must jump – with an existential leap – into the Void, leaving the scientist, the philosopher, and even the psychologist, bewildered and annoyed, behind. True, the 'Gods' of Mahayana Buddhism are no more than concepts as we discuss them. Suchness, the Void and the Store-Consciousness of Mind-Only, all these are concepts and no more until we make them more by knowing them to be true as distinct from knowing about them as the material of thinking.

But the intellect must be developed and fully used. In Nature's staircase to perfection no step may be left out. We must learn to think to the very end of thought, to think deeply into thoughts that are on the face of them nonsense, to understand, so far as thought can help us, what Dr Suzuki calls Zen logic, that A is A because A is not-A, and to see, as he puts it, why God created the Universe. But while striving to catch the butterfly of Zen in the net of reason we must know that the task is hopeless. Nor, as I said elsewhere, will it yield to the bird-lime of paradox, though some in this way have caught its tail.

How, then, *do* we know? By the intuition, in the East known as Buddhi, the function which Jung described in his famous diagram as pairing with the senses, even as we are all more developed in the intellect or the emotions. Note that this intuition is direct and im-mediate in experience. By it we know, as im-mediately as a hand which picks up a red-hot instrument knows pain. The senses and the intuition *know*; the emotions and the intellect work on material provided by the other two. This perhaps explains the emphasis on sense experience in Zen training. When we can really see the flower, hear the rain, touch the velvet of the rose, and do so merging in their Suchness, we are knowing Truth directly. Meanwhile the intuition is a function which we all possess but which very few of us can use at will. It must be developed, and this can only be done by use. We must read the literature that rouses it, seek its voice in meditation, obey it when it comes. It is the inspiration of the artist and poet, the high awareness of the greatest scientist, thinker, musician, mathematician, statesman or mystical devotee. Suddenly the great mind 'sees' what it had not seen before, but sees with eyes beyond the plane of thinking. But it must be wooed on its own plane, roused by one's own efforts. Here is Zen, and here we must find it. For the intuition is the function of direct contact with All-Mind; it is therefore the instrument by which the part makes contact with the Whole. Satori is a flash of intuition deep enough and wide enough to break the barriers of thought in the individual mind, and to let the Whole flood into the part, the relative fragment 'see', for a moment of no-time, the Absolute.

But its plane cannot be described. It is as foolish to tie labels round the neck of Truth as to throw adjectives at the sunset. Truth may smile, but she will not be amused, and the sunset *is*, whatever we shout about it. We must therefore rise to the plane of Zen and not attempt to describe it, or to limit it in any way.

It may be that these thousands of words to prove that Zen lies beyond thinking are quite unnecessary, but as shown in the correspondence set out in my *Zen Comes West*, the average student, though he pay lip service to this statement, continues to search for Zen in books and lectures and recorded Sayings. He will not face the fact that it lies in his own mind, but at a level above the highest thought he has then achieved, or ever will. At least let us now look further at the plane where, say the Masters, Zen *is* to be found.

It is a world beyond the limits of reasoning. A proposition may therefore be true although it is nonsense, i.e. non-sense, beyond the limits of our conventional view of sense. 'A is A because A is not-A' is nonsense, but pure Zen. Poets know this kingdom and the greatest verse proceeds from it; children for a while live in it. Mystics reach it and try to describe it, but they have to use symbol and analogy and poetry to do it at all. Jung spoke of the numinosity of religion, the numinous, or superphenomenal region of the mind, which ignores the rational for it *knows* beyond it. For this awareness is essentially beyond the four-square field of logic and reasoning. The Prajna, Wisdom, that we seek is pāra-mitā, 'gone beyond'; hence the name of that supernal body of literature described earlier, the Prajna-pāra-mitā, the Wisdom that has gone beyond. None can describe this Wisdom; 'even Buddhas do but point the Way'.

Yet no hard line can be drawn between the planes of consciousness; all are facets of an indivisible and immensely complex whole. As awareness rises in terms of synthesis, all differences tend to 'blend and blur', as Rupert Brooke said of the centuries, in moments of Zen seeing. More and more is included in the field of consciousness, a new harmony of discordant factors once seen at enmity. Alan Watts speaks of 'a state of inner feeling in which oppositions have become mutually co-operative instead of mutually exclusive', and this new sense can cheerfully include in its embrace a contradictory mixture of thought and emotion, sense and nonsense, true and as obviously untrue, and even the old enemies, good and evil.

'Let the mind alight nowhere.' This is the ideal of all Zen training, achieved when at last attachment to thought is ended, and ideas may be used as tools without becoming so many fetters. The change will cause a change in reading material. Those books alone will satisfy which 'ring a bell' in the intuition, and if this is their effect it matters not what they are. A few are listed in Letter 39 of my *Zen Comes West*; here I would only mention the few great scriptures of the world, usually small in volume, such as the Heart Sutra, the Voice of the Silence, the Tao Te Ching, the Bhagavad Gita and the fourth Gospel. The sensitive student will soon begin to choose among modern publications, between those writers who speak Zen and those who only talk about it. In the former class Dr. Suzuki towers above all others, for he alone of all Zen masters has full knowledge of the English language in which to express his enlightenment. Yet many in the West are having their 'experience', great or small, and it is useful exercise in the development of the intuition to decide where descriptions of such an experience merely record an event on the psychic plane, and where it is a genuine flash of Zen. In the same way the student will distinguish between Zen talk and mere argument, for the latter gets nowhere at all. Paradox becomes a means of self-expression, and in some cases the only one, and there is a new sense of tolerance which is born of a dawning vision of things as they are before they split into two. If both sides of the coin can be seen, as it were, at once, as two sides of a whole, it is easier to be tolerant of the views expressed by those who see but one of them. The pairs of opposites are one by one resolved in terms of opposition, from Self and no-self, or predestination and freewill, to the ultimate pairs of positive/negative, subject/object, and Zen logic, which is explained when we see 'why God created the Universe'.

Now is the wakening of the new Zen consciousness, a willingness to drop the exhausting attempt to resolve dualities in a concept which unites them. This is not possible, for any concept, however uniting, still has its opposite somewhere, is still incomplete. As Jung points out, no problem is ever solved on its own plane; the third factor is beyond conception. Even the pursuit of Zen is folly, for *I* am pursuing *Zen* – two things, I and Zen! Hence the only usable phrase, Non-duality, not one, not two. As I said in *Zen Comes West*, 'It is not one, not two, not both and not neither. You can't get hold of it. *Don't try*. For while the part sees the Whole there is no Zen, for there are still two things, the part and the Whole. Zen awareness must be an expansion of consciousness beyond all knowledge of any kind and beyond all process. It must include the unconscious in this consciousness. This is not my theory, for Jung says it and Suzuki says it, in different terms but without reference to each other. This only is the true Self, the babe that shall grow and become the universe.' For this babe is already enlightened, but unlike us that write and read these words, it knows it. But how to help it know? That is the problem of the Zen master, and to make this clear has been the object of this chapter. Why does the Zen master talk in riddles and paradox, talk nonsense, do silly things and even use violence on the pupil who comes to him? Not to show off, or because he is too lazy to explain. He *cannot* explain what is Zen, yet he must in some way help the increasing tension in the student's mind to explode in a flash of Satori, a KNOWING beyond all thinking, a position at rest beyond and above and yet within the opposites and all duality.

CHAPTER NINE

IN A ZEN MONASTERY

As this work is primarily intended for those who seek to tread the way of Zen in the West, little space need be given to the life of the Zen monk in the East, and the monasteries in which he carries out his training. Yet if Roshis, trained Zen teachers, are to come to Europe to teach us, we should know the conditions of life from which they come; and if Westerners are to spend their savings in reaching Japan for training, they should know to what conditions they are going. Some of these conditions cannot be reproduced in Europe; some should not be, a matter to be further considered under the heading of Zen comes West. They include, on the physical plane, great beauty, such wealth of beauty in all things large and small as may be found in no other place on earth. In personal terms, a deliberately ordered life, a blend of physical hard work, mental and emotional self-restraint, and fiercely dedicated purpose pursued with unremitting vigour for twenty-four hours a day. Yet the whole suffused with a lightness of touch and unlimited laughter, ever ready to burst out on the least occasion.

The site of the monastery itself is beautiful, whether on the fringes of a town or deep in the country. Always there are glorious trees about it, and when possible running water. The whole domain, and some cover many acres, is spotlessly clean, and each building is itself an example of that exquisite chastity of taste in which the finest of Japanese art excels. Nothing is redundant, nothing unsightly; all has a purpose or it would not be there. There are many buildings in the compound. All large monasteries have at least a Hondo, or main building, a Zendo, where the monks meditate and sleep at night, a Bell Tower, the Abbot's quarters which often include a Guests' wing, and a Gate-house which is sometimes a noble building in its own right. Nowadays there is usually a treasure-house of concrete, to store valuables safe from the ever-present risk of fire, but often this concrete shell is itself covered with a screen of something less offensive to the eye. In each compound there are smaller temples, each self-contained, but all under the control of the Abbot or Kancho of the monastery. Nearly all large establishments are called -Ji, as Myoshin-ji, one of the main temples of the Rinzai Zen School. Smaller units may be called -In, while -An is used for a smaller unit still, as Ryosen-an, a sub-temple refounded by Mrs. Ruth Sasaki in Daitoku-ji for Western students of Zen.

The staff of a monastery school, other than the Abbot, so far as the study of Zen is concerned consists of the all-important Roshi and the Jikijitsu or head-monk who rules the Zendo. The pupils include those who intend to be monks for life, those who intend when their training is over to be the heads of village temples, somewhat equivalent to the Western 'parish priest', and those who enter for a period of self-training before returning to the world.

The Sodo, or school within the monastery, has terms like any other school, but the pupils never forget their koan study, if they have reached that level, even in vacation. It was hard to be admitted to the monastery at all; once in, they have no other thought than success. For it is still today hard to gain admittance, and the monastic schools do not accept a novice unless he proves himself to be suitable material. He is taught no doctrine, but set to breathing for long hours in the Zendo and elsewhere, until he can concentrate on breathing alone to the satisfaction of his immediate master. Only when he can 'sit' in every sense of the term, properly, easily and for long periods, and has learnt to breathe, in the sense given above, will he be admitted to the Roshi for a formal interview, and if the Roshi is satisfied, accepted as his pupil.

The life is strenuous. Throughout the long Japanese winter

there is no heating in the buildings whatsoever, by night or day, and the conditions at 4 a.m., with a foot of snow in the courtyard, and only a paper screen for a window, may be imagined. The food is simple and monotonous, and for the European, as for many of the monks, insufficient. There is little comfort, and the hours are so long that few get sufficient sleep. The intensive effort knows little relaxation. Books are discouraged, and there is no 'entertainment' as we in the West understand the term.

Why, then, do young men even today seek entry to a life of these conditions? Because they want what the training and, so they believe, that training alone will supply. Their intellectual power will vary, as will their knowledge of the Scriptures. But mere intellectual study is discouraged. The source of the Roshi's sermons is generally that endless reservoir of Mondo, the rapid exchange of question/answer recorded from past ages, in China or Japan, as taking place between master and pupil, just anywhere where the two may come together in the course of the day. As already described, many of these Collections have survived, the best known to the West being the Mumonkan (the Gateless Gate) and the Hekigan Roku (Blue Cliff Records) both of China.

The heart of a Zen monastery is the Zen-do, where the pupils meditate, each on his padded mat, six feet by three, and here he sleeps at night. This is his only 'room', and here he keeps his possessions, so few that they go into a large silk square and thence into a locker at his head. Meals are taken elsewhere, in silence, after special chanting in which all join.

Western students must overcome the agony of long hours of sitting cross-legged, in the Eastern sense of this term, which, in the later stages of training, implies the full 'lotus' posture in which the sole of each foot appears upward on the opposite thigh. They must also know enough Japanese to converse rapidly and fluently with the Roshi on their progress in Koan study, and this facility is not easily learnt. Even the Japanese student finds the third requirement difficult, to drop discursive thinking, so to still the mind that the unconscious may enter consciousness and the first stage towards No-thought be achieved.

For there is no escape for the inquiring mind, into thought and feeling, into projections onto Gods and other Saviours, and the Roshi's task is primarily to drive the developing power of the will back on to itself for a realization of the Buddha-mind within. For Zen Buddhism is *jiriki*, salvation by self-Power, as distinct from *tariki*, salvation by Other-power. It is self-effort all the way, and even the Master can but guide the pupil's footsteps and keep him on the 'way' that he has chosen. For within the Way of Zen are divers 'ways' (Japanese *Do* from the Chinese *Tao*). Archery is one of them, as we know from Eugen Herrigel's now famous work, *Zen in the Art of Archery*. Others are Judo, Kendo (Fencing), Ikebana (Flower-arrangement), now well known in Europe through the writing and lecturing of Stella Coe, herself a qualified Master of this exquisite art. Other forms of Japanese culture are steeped in Zen even if not Zen-created. The famous Tea Ceremony, the building of a garden, Haiku, the Japanese seventeen syllable poem, and calligraphy, all these can be used as 'ways' to the One and to that which lies beyond it. First comes technique, so mastered that it is forgotten; then comes the 'use' of it. Nor need the list of ways be closed. As Trevor Leggett points out at the end of his *First Zen Reader*, typing may well be included, or any craft where the same considerations apply!

In Soto Zen the 'sitting' or Za-zen is held to be sufficient in itself, for in it the pupil learns that he is already enlightened, that he *is* the Buddha, with the Buddha-nature only waiting to be realized. The life, the sitting and Buddhahood are seen as one. But this is a School of which we know too little, and though in a sense far simpler in form than the more dynamic Rinzai Zen, it is in fact so subtle that only a genuine mystical awareness will prevent the practice degenerating into just sitting, in which nothing happens at all.

Yet the goal is the same enlightenment. The first peep is known as Kensho, a deeper experience as Satori; far beyond the latter is the Buddha's Enlightenment. Yet the experience is not the goal of Zen endeavour, for the will to achieve anything defeats itself; there is still someone who wants to achieve something, and there is in truth no seeker, no seeking and no sought – all are illusions, veils about the face of Reality. Even when achieved this satori is not the end of Zen; rather it is the beginning of the final path, and all that preceded it is but an approach to the entrance of that Path which is in truth the mind that treads it. 'I am the Way . . .' said Jesus the Christ. 'Look within; thou *art* Buddha,' says *The Voice of the Silence*. And again, 'Thou canst not tread the Path until thou hast become that Path thyself.' This is indeed far from the 'bright idea', the witty use of words beloved of 'Beat Zen' enthusiasts. For here is the dedication of the total man to a Path which has no turning and on which there is no turning back. At the beginning lies man as he thinks he is, unaware of what he truly is; at the end lies the full development of Man as the universe in miniature with a Mind which is one with All-Mind.

Meanwhile we have two men face to face in a small room in the monastery, the Roshi and the particular pupil with whose problems he is then concerned. Formal bows are made and acknowledged; after that there is nothing in the world for the pupil save his agony of will, and the man whose whole endeavour is to help him resolve it. What can the Roshi do to help? He is a man not only enlightened but further trained, after a long period of 'maturing', in the difficult science of teaching what he knows. But teaching involves method, technique, a means, or a thousand different means, to the end. But here the means must be themselves beyond duality, or at least beyond the usual methods which employ a pair of the opposites. This rules out conversation as generally understood. There can be no 'explanation' of Reality; still less is it amenable to argument. The pupil needs far more than words 'about it and about'. He has had all these from lectures, sermons, books. What he wants is an almost physical pull or push to achieve an almost physical need, the break-out of the desperate chicken from the egg. Picture, then, the pupil struggling in a net, clambering through a narrow window, tearing the final curtains from an eye that yearns to see. What *can* the wise, experienced, deeply compassionate teacher do to help the pupil in the hell of effort which was his own not all that time ago?

The answer cannot lie in the field of rational behaviour. The countless stories of what Masters did in the past and are doing today will therefore not be rational, and probably not helpful to the seeker now writhing in the coils of his koan. Hence the stories of a blow, a laugh, a foolish gesture, a silly joke, silence or a bellow of apparent rage. If they 'work', if they succeed in snapping the last link between self and Reality, does it matter what the Master does? The violence may do what years of gentle encouragement had failed to do. Again and again, we read of passionate seekers flung out of the monastery itself by a 'furious' Roshi, and told to seek Truth elsewhere. The seeker seeks, elsewhere, and years may elapse before he returns, bearing his triumph with him. To complain of the Master's treatment? No, to thank him for the violence which sent him back into the deeps of his own mind. Where encouragement may only sap the will the fierceness of a Bodhidharma may rouse it to final victory.

Yet the Roshi is not always fierce. When the pupil's need, as he sees it, is for encouragement and sympathy his need will be supplied. The Bodhisattva mind of the teacher is full of a thousand 'devices' (*hoben*) and infinite patience in helping the pupil to get free. The demonstration of Truth, if need be for years, goes on unceasingly, but the Roshi helps in his own way, based on his own experience, and the Western student may not see for a while that he provides what the 'patient' needs, which is not always what the pupil in his ignorance desires. For the Roshi stands to his pupil as Prajna/

Karuna, wisdom which spills into compassionate 'right' action; and compassion, which is wisdom using the right means to the mutually needed end.

These Mondo, or stories of Master/pupil interviews, must be rightly used when taken at second-hand. If a Master, when asked the meaning of Bodhidharma's coming from the West, says 'a pot of tea', or 'Ask the gardener', or 'The One is the One but what is One plus One?', these answers may serve, at the time, to give that questioner what he needed, but it does not follow that another, asking the same question, will receive any of those answers, or any at all. The whole interview between pupil and Master lies beyond the realm of reason, and logic is left behind. The pupil asks; the Master answers. The unutterable 'moment' has passed for ever; *that* Master and *that* pupil will never meet again.

This, I take it, is why these Mondo when published as Collections are followed by the comments of the collector, and sometimes by another as well. These comments are to the intellect confusion worse confounded; if possible they madden the mind still further, but that is their purpose. They are meant to stop the student from attempting to drag them down to the level of thought in order to unravel them into the strands of reasoning.

What, then, is the use of these Mondo? They rouse the intuition to greater functioning, and break the mind's habit of rational thought. They tease, irritate, incite to higher solution, bait the will to fresh endeavour. Used as the subject of meditation, in formal 'sitting' or all the day, they stop the mind from thinking and rouse it to *know*. Here are some of them; to add further comment on their 'meaning' would be lending a match-light to the sun, and therefore useless, and certainly clouding the eyes still further from the light of Zen.

CHAPTER TEN

THE SAYINGS OF ZEN MASTERS

As will now be apparent, the whole system of Zen training is based upon the Roshi, his nature, functions and method of teaching. The word means old teacher, old in the sense of venerable. He is the spiritual head of the monastery, but leaves the control of temporal affairs to the Abbot. He may be young or old, gentle or fierce in technique, learned as the world holds learning or only skilled in Zen. But before he is given the 'seal' of his position as Roshi he must have achieved considerable enlightenment, have had that experience 'matured' by time and study, and have been taught to teach. His function towards his pupils is part teacher, part priest and part psychiatrist. He receives in his total self the onslaught of numerous highly charged, impatient, tense and determined minds, determined to 'get it'. To them he is the last hope, the one man who can help them break through to their own enlightenment; to him they are fellow beings whom he loves as such, and would 'save' in the best way possible from their no longer tolerable bondage. He has to rouse their internal pressure to its highest pitch, to keep it so through doubt, exhaustion and despair, and to guide the fierce advance towards success. When necessary he must reduce the pressure lest it burst out in the wrong direction, and this is one of the most important of his duties. But he must close every avenue of escape by the thinking mind which, now desperate, strives to avoid its immanent surrender. This mind will attempt all manner of tricks and devices, pseudo-solutions to the problem, set imitations of others' solutions, or 'transference' as the psychiatrist of the West calls it, but the Roshi is old in all of them. Sitting fast on the heights of his own awareness, he observes with heart of compassion the furious struggles of the pupil at his feet. He will not descend to the level of his intellect; the pupil must be made to rise to the plane of Non-duality in which alone he will 'see' the world afresh with newly-awakened eyes. As already shown, he cannot explain or describe; still less will he argue. Whatever the pupil says will be wrong, because partial. Thought must be stilled, or slain, or dropped, not as an instrument well forged and noble of its kind, but as a limitation of life, as a net or cage wherein life, stopped in its essential movement, is not allowed to 'walk on'. But the master claims no 'authority' for his answers, nor for those of his predecessors to whom the same questions, representing the same problems, have been put for fifteen hundred years. There is no solution to a Koan, no right 'answer' to a question. A master when asked, who is the Buddha?' may answer 'mud', or 'next Wednesday', or 'yes' or even 'an Indian princeling of the sixth century B.C.', and each will be the right answer for that pupil in that state of mind at that time. Hence the value of recorded answers to questions is limited, but within those limits the study of any one of them may spark off the longed-for experience.

The relation between the Koan and the Mondo is intimate. The Koan, pronounced Kō-ān, is a word or phrase of no intellectual meaning, such as *mu*, literally No, being Joshu's answer to the question, 'Has a dog Buddha-nature?', or 'What is the sound of one hand clapping?', or 'What was your original (primordial) face before your parents were born?' The mind wraps itself round the given koan by night and day for weeks and months on end. First, the intellect tries to solve it, and fails. Then it is sucked dry of symbolism, analogy, and metaphor. And so through endless methods the mind tries to solve the insoluble. Meanwhile the tension grows; the engine of thought is forced down a narrowing corridor with high walls on either side – only to face a high wall at the end. The pressure grows; the pupil sweats and is sleepless with effort, while the master watches, as a doctor over a woman in travail, helping where he can, controlling where he must, until the experience comes, and he is the first to 'recognize' its genuine nature. But the koan system has its dangers. In the absence of a highly qualified and trained Roshi to assist the pupil there is no one to say when he is on or off the beam in his endeavours, and none to say when he has genuinely 'solved' his koan. More important, there is no one to protect him from raising such a head of steam, as one student calls it, that without very experienced guidance the whole mind may crack, meaning temporary or permanent insanity. In the absence of a Roshi, therefore, I refuse to make use of the koan technique in the Zen Class of the Buddhist Society, and do not advise its use. Nor is it necessary for Zen training. For centuries it was unknown in Zen practice, and it is not used in the Soto Zen School which is numerically even larger than the Rinzai School with which we are here concerned. For a long while the native grandeur of the Roshi's mind was enough to assist his pupils to break through, and five hundred years of successive masters had no need of this or any other definite technique. Each had his own way of helping the pupil to smash the cage of thought, and to reach that point before the One was born from the Void, and the One became the infinitely various two. The koan system is no more than a device, a means to an end and a very powerful one. But though the West may lack for a long while resident Roshis capable of applying it safely, we need not despair. We must find our own technique to the same end.

The Mondo, question/answer, explains itself. As they are recorded moments of conversation between pupil and master, they are almost infinite in range and form, and vast in number. Some are physical demonstrations to illustrate the master's point. A teacher noticed that a pupil sat all day long in the crossed-leg position, meditating. 'What are you seeking in this way?' he asked. 'To become a Buddha.' The master took up a piece of brick and began to polish it on a stone. 'What are you doing, master?' 'Making a mirror.' 'You won't make a mirror by polishing a brick.' 'And no amount of sitting cross-legged will make you a Buddha,' replied the master. But the story ends by the pupil asking what he should do instead. Said the master, 'It is like driving a cart. When it won't move, do you whip the cart or the ox?'

A dramatic way of making a point was used by a master who, finding it very cold in a shrine, took a wooden image off the altar and used it for fuel in the stove. The keeper of the shrine was horrified and protested at length, but the master, unabashed, was poking about in the ashes. 'What are you looking for?' asked the keeper. 'For sariras*,' said the master. 'But how do you hope to find them in the ashes of a wooden Buddha?' asked the keeper. 'If none are found in it may I have the other two wooden Buddhas for my fire?' Here is at least a powerful way of stopping the worship of relics, and more, any great regard for any 'thing' whatsoever.

A similar story may be usefully quoted to oneself a dozen times a day. Two monks, on the way home to their monastery, came to a ford where they found a young girl hesitating to cross lest she spoil her clothes. One of the monks without a word just picked her up and carried her over. The other monk remonstrated for the rest of their journey home while the first, wrapped in his meditation, made no reply. At the entrance to the monastery he heard his colleague muttering fiercely, 'You – a monk – and a girl in your arms. What a dreadful thing to do!' Said the first monk, 'Are *you* still carrying that girl in your arms? *I* put her down at the ford.'

Some of the mondo are easy to understand in the sense that their meaning can be translated into normal prose. A master had as a disciple a high government official, who was one day late in arriving. He apologized and explained that he had been watching a polo match. 'Were the men tired?' asked the master. 'Yes, master.' 'Were the horses tired?' 'Yes, master.' 'Is the wooden post here tired too?' The official could not answer, but in the middle of the night he rose and hurried back to the

* Small objects like pebbles said to be found in the ashes of Saints.

masters' room. 'Ask me again,' he pleaded. The master put the question again and the answer was, of course, 'Yes, master.' For, as a later commentator pointed out, unless the post was tired too there could be no tiredness anywhere.

More difficult, but still within the reach of the intellect, is the story of the wild geese (more accurately, a wild duck) that flew away. A master and pupil were out walking when a wild duck flew up in front of them. Asked the master, 'What was that?' The pupil answered, 'A wild duck.' 'Where did it go?' asked the master. 'It has just flown away,' The master gave his pupil's nose a violent tweak, at which he cried out in pain. 'Flown away, has it? Why it has been here all the time.' The pain of the tweak succeeded.

This story illustrates, incidentally, how a question demanding an answer might be put at any time of the day or night by master to pupil, or the other way round. Any 'incident' or theme was good enough to test the pupil's growing awareness of Non-duality, or to prove to him that it was not growing at all.

Here is a harder story, on which generations have worked in the last thousand years. It shows again how the ripened mind may be brought to the explosion point by the most trivial incident.

A monk called on his teacher, and was there when night fell. He rose to go and, lifting up the screen, went out. Finding it was dark he turned and said, 'It is dark outside.' The master lit a candle-lantern and gave it him. Just as he was about to take it the master stopped and blew it out. The pupil had his sudden enlightenment.

Comparable is the famous story of the goose in the bottle. A visitor put to a master the following problem. A man kept a goose in a bottle till it grew so large that it couldn't get out any more. How to get the goose out without hurting the goose or breaking the bottle? The master said to his visitor. 'Officer!' 'Yes,' answered the officer. 'There,' said the master, 'it's out!' We are not told if the officer 'got it' from this reply.

Mondo may be classified and grouped in a hundred ways, for the store of them available is legion. Here is a brief selection which will suffice to show the variety and the way in which any student can use them, to move at least in the direction of the same experience.

A famous stanza by a master of the T'ang Dynasty of China reads,

'Empty-handed I go, and behold, the spade is in my hands.
I walk on foot, yet am riding on the back of an ox;
When I pass over the bridge
Lo, the water flows not; it is the bridge that flows.'

Again, a monk asked his master, 'How is it when a man brings nothing with him?' 'Throw it away,' shouted the master. 'But what shall he throw away if he has not anything at all?' 'Then carry it along,' said the master. Which reminds one of the pupil who boasted that he had achieved a state of emptiness of mind. 'Now I have no idea,' he claimed. 'Why stagger about under the burden of this concept, "no idea"?' asked the master mildly. A Roshi carries with him a stick to walk with, and a kind of fly-whisk. Both are frequently used to illustrate his point. A master held up his staff and said, 'If you call this a staff you are caught (by its name). If you do not call it a staff you contradict (reality). So what do you call it?' Commenting on this, Mumon, the collector of the Mumonkan or 'Gateless Gate' collection, says:

'Holding up a staff
He cried, "Come on, come on!"
Faced with the alternative of being caught or contradicting,
Even the Buddhas and the Patriarchs would beg for their lives.'

The spirit of urgency is intense. Again and again the master, after putting a question cries, 'Speak, Speak!' For the answer must be spontaneous and immediate. Any time-lag exposes the monk's inability to reply from his Essence of Mind, and betrays the thinking mind at work to create an answer. The speed of question/answer is instantaneous. Only thus is thinking cut out and the pupil led to that 'moment' before division was born and the Void was stained with duality. Thus another master is recorded as holding up his staff to a group of pupils. 'If you call it a staff, you assert. If you deny that it is a staff you negate. Without affirmation or denial, speak, speak!' A monk came forward, took the staff and threw it to the floor. That at least was his answer, without affirming or denying. What is yours? In the olden days there was a master who offered, and if he could reach them gave, thirty blows with his stick to all of his monks who could not answer such a question. 'Beyond assertion and beyond denial,' he would say, 'Quick, quick – speak, or thirty blows'. For thus only can experience be expressed, beyond the duality which in the experience itself is transcended. When the Master of a famous monastery wanted a dragon painted on the ceiling of its principal building, and the artist complained that he had never seen a dragon, he was sent away again and again with his complaint unanswered. In the end the old man shouted at him 'Fool! *Become* the dragon!' And apparently he did, for the dragon is there to this day and fearsome indeed to see.

The demonstration of inward understanding can be infinitely various. One of the best-known instances occurred when an Abbot-Roshi had to select a master for a new monastery. He summoned the monks, and placing a pitcher on the floor said, 'If you cannot call this a pitcher, what would you call it?' Said the chief monk, who hoped to get the appointment, 'You can't call it a stump.' But the cook got up and kicked the pitcher over. He got the job.

Zen lives in facts and hates abstraction. Hence much of the master's time is spent in bringing to earth the thought-filled mind of the pupil. The way of Zen, as Bodhidharma himself declared, is vitally direct. All intermediate thoughts and ideas conceal the truth, and spoil the direct transmission of spiritual decision to the perfect and im-mediate act. When a new arrival demurred at the bathing arrangements in a monastery, the answer came, 'Just a dip, and no why,' which can be applied by all of us every moment of the day. This is perhaps why R. H. Blyth has better than any other translator caught the spirit of a famous Haiku, the seventeen-syllable Japanese poem, by Basho. The last line literally reads 'the sound of the water'. Here is Blyth's, and he spent many years in Korean Zen monasteries before he went to live in Japan.

> The old pond
> A frog jumps in –
> Plop!

The purpose of all Zen training, as will now be clear, is the breakthrough to Non-duality, a personal, direct experience of what is to us the Absolute. As shown in Mahayana literature the state of Nirvana, the end of self in SELF, is to be achieved in, because it only exists in, Samsara, the world of 'becoming'; the two are one, two modes of one state which from the human point of view is one experience. It follows that this glimpse of the Absolute is to be sought here and now, not only in the mystical state of Here and Now, because there is nought else, but literally in doing what we are doing now, be it meditation, earning a living, or washing-up. It follows further, and this is a step of profound importance, that whatever we are doing at any moment is a situation of importance, and any two are of equal importance. If it ought to be done, let it be done, whether it is writing a letter or going to sleep. In the situation now before one, and nowhere else, will Zen be found, or not found at all. Hence the master's perpetual effort to drive back the seeker to the only point where he will find It, whatever that is – in the deeps of his own mind, his Essence of Mind, which is No-mind. 'Every day is a good day,' said a great master. Every day offers innumerable opportunities for right action, in the ultimate sense of 'Right', as on the Noble Eightfold Path of basic Buddhism.

A good example is the story of a visitor who asked a master, 'Do you discipline yourself in the Buddha-teaching?' 'Certainly

I do,' said the master. 'How do you exercise yourself?' asked the visitor. 'When I am hungry I eat, when I am tired I sleep,' replied the master. 'But that is what everybody does. Are they exercising themselves in the same way as you?' 'No,' said the master, most emphatically, 'because when they eat they do not eat, but are thinking of other things, allowing themselves to be disturbed by thoughts; when they sleep, they do not sleep, but dream of a thousand and one things. That is the difference.'

In one sense the pursuit of Zen is simple indeed. When a famous master was asked by a novice to instruct him the master replied, 'Have you had your breakfast yet?' 'I have had my breakfast, thank you,' replied the novice. 'Then wash your bowl,' said the master. And that was sufficient for the novice. So was this answer to another inquirer, obviously complaining of the extremes of temperature to be endured in a Zen monastery. 'Cold and heat come upon us,' he said. 'How should one avoid these extremes?' The master replied, 'Why not go where there is neither cold nor heat?' 'Is there such a place?' inquired the complainer. 'Certainly,' said the master. 'When cold, be thoroughly cold and when hot be hot through and through!'

In this acceptance, complete and thorough acceptance of facts as they are, lies much of the secret of Zen. It eliminates the foolish sense of self, and is a long step towards Zen 'seeing', that is, seeing things as they truly are, empty of substance and without more significance than we decide to give them.

A phrase which is often quoted to describe this sense of the here and now is in No. 19 of the Mumonkan. It reads:

'What is Tao (Or Truth or God or Zen)?
Ordinary mind is Tao.
Should we try to get it?
As soon as you try you miss it . . .'

But this 'ordinary mind' or 'everyday mind' is not in a state of Zen until the owner of the mind discovers it. This popular mondo does not mean that if we carry on life as usual we shall sooner or later arrive at Zen. Nor does it mean that in the midst of wordly activities we can chase the tail of Zen as it flits about at the margin of consciousness. To be in the world, yet not clinging to or forming attachments for the dust of the world, such is the way of the true Zen student. But the ceasing to form attachments needs more than a single resolution of the will; it is the whole way of the path of Zen, its beginning, its middle and its end.

This famous phrase implies, too, that it is useless to look elsewhere for the Essence of Mind. It is forever Here and Now and concerned with This, in the mystical sense, and no Saviour can supply it. Nowhere but here can the answer be obtained, not in heaven, not in ceremony, nor in the Scriptures. Above all, not in concepts and splendid formulae. Asked by an earnest student, 'What is my self?' the master replied, 'What would you do with a self?' and in those words revealed the pure light of Zen. We have all, need nothing, are everything. And all is one, just one, not two. Always the master drives this home. It was the great Joshu – he who said '*Mu*' to the question about the Buddha in a dog – who said all that need be said on this subject. A monk in search of the 'One word of Truth' which would reveal the universe to his inquiring mind asked Joshu, 'What is the one word?' Asked Joshu, 'What do you say?' 'What is the one word?' repeated the foolish inquirer. 'You make it two,' was the reply.

These, then, are some of the mondo which to our Western minds are immediately helpful. But there are hundreds which to us are meaningless. Sometimes the cause is not our fault. The 'point' of the dialogue is often lost to us in allusions and analogies of which we have no knowledge. But others are meant to be beyond the intellect, if only to bring back the questioner from his intellectual heaven of thinking. When Joshu was asked why the Patriarch Bodhidharma came from the West – a stock conundrum used as an opening gambit –

Joshu answered, 'The oak tree in the garden.' And when two masters questioned each other, how the listeners struggled to attain the level at which they talked!

These mondo, then, are the raw material for our own unceasing effort to attain the experience in which they were born. Some are easy for us, some at present impossible. Yet all are useful, and as the years go by we suddenly 'see' what before was meaningless. At least we can do ourselves no harm to worry at our chosen mondo, until we crack its form and extract the juice of enlightenment. Hundreds are now available in English; when these are exhausted there will be time to ask for more.

CHAPTER ELEVEN

THE WRITINGS OF ZEN MASTERS

IT is a far cry from the Mahayana Scriptures quoted in Chapter Six to a mondo such as, 'Who was the Buddha?' 'I hear what you say.' Both are difficult for the Western mind to assimilate, for in modern parlance our minds have been 'conditioned' so very differently. Sometimes the Sermons of the masters make it easier to approach the supreme experience from which both Scripture and mondo came, for they present the listeners' minds with an understandable theme for meditation. Sometimes the Sermon is a commentary on a recorded mondo; sometimes the theme is taken from a Scriptural text, as in the West. Here is a brief selection from the writings of four famous masters. It matters not for our purpose if in fact the writing was that of a disciple recording his master's words.

We can begin with the greatest figure in the history of Zen Buddhism, the sixth Patriarch, Hui-neng. The Founder of the Zen movement was Bodhidharma, who brought the essentially Zen methods to China in the sixth century. But it was only with Hui-neng that the new teaching shed the last of its Indian wrappings and became essentially Chinese. The more we learn of Hui-neng and his place in Far-eastern religious history, the larger the man becomes. In *The Zen Doctrine of No-Mind* Dr. Suzuki attempted to do justice to his teaching, but much remains to be said. One of his greatest pupils was Shen-hui, whose Sayings are themselves about to be published in English, thanks to the labours of Dr. Richard Chi. We will draw on these Sayings to explain why Hui-neng called his the Sudden School as distinct from the Gradual School of his rival pupil of the fifth Patriarch, Shen-hsiu. Then we will turn to Huang-Po, the great teacher of Lin-Chi (Jap. Rinzai) who was the spiritual father of the present Rinzai sect of Japan. Finally, we must find room for the first part of the famous song of the third Patriarch, Seng-t'san, 'On Trust in the Heart', which of all Zen writings is, with the Heart Sutra and the Mumonkan, the most popular in Japan today.

Hui-neng was indeed the true Founder of Zen Buddhism. Although he refused to transmit further the Robe and the Bowl which Bodhi-dharma handed down through the Chinese Patriarchs for two hundred years, he left such a body of enlightened men to succeed him that the movement soon spread throughout China and is today the most influential school in Japan. He included his autobiography in his famous Platform Sutra (Tan-ching) and we therefore know what he regarded as the basic principles of Zen. He stated all of them in one tremendous phrase, 'From the first not a thing is'; all else flows from this supernal statement. He spoke, of course, from his own experience, but he was voicing the wisdom of the whole range of the Prajnaparamita literature. (See Chapter Six.) He took his stand on the Unconscious, the primordial No-Mind, the Whole expressed through the medium of one partial mind. This 'self-conscious Unconscious' is known as Prajna, and is the key-term of Hui-neng's teaching.

As this is related to Hui-neng's insistence on the 'sudden' nature of Zen experience, we may consider his teachings on the two great themes together. Prajna, then, is the sudden, im-mediate awareness of Non-duality, of the non-relative which to us is the Absolute. It is beyond time and all imitation. Dhyana, on the other hand, is a form of meditation in time and duality. Its primary aim is level-mindedness, a stilling of the waves of thought. 'When the mind is disturbed the multiplicity of things is produced; when the mind is quieted, they disappear.' Dhyana is the process of this quieting. Dhyana leads to the third term here considered, Samadhi, a condition of consciousness when the waves are stilled. The use of Dhyana to achieve Samadhi is a gradual process; the break-through into Prajna consciousness is, and clearly must be, sudden.

Hui-neng clearly distinguished, and for the first time, the process of Dhyana and the achievement of Satori in Prajna, supreme Wisdom which, when attained, manifests in endless deeds of Karuna, compassion, by which alone the Wisdom knows itself as such and is visible to the eyes of men. Yet though Dhyana must be distinguished from Prajna, Prajna cannot be achieved without Dhyana, meditation. Without Dhyana no Prajna would be attained; without the existence of Prajna no success in Dhyana would be possible. They are two modes of one awareness.

All this is not merely technical, still less a matter of doctrine. The whole is made practical in a typically Zen way in the story, already quoted, of the meditating pupil and the brick. Just as the Master would never make a mirror by polishing a brick, so the pupil would never become a Buddha by sitting in the spiritually comfortable condition of Samadhi. Sooner or later the enormous energy must be developed and piled up which one day, in a supreme 'moment', will be totally expended in the existential leap into the Absolute. Meanwhile the emphasis on Dhyana or Prajna is different and complementary in the two main schools of Zen; the Soto, with its quiet sitting and emphasis on the mind's serenity, and the Rinzai, with its emphasis on the leap. Both aim at the same state of enlightenment, when the Unconscious 'No-Mind' of non-duality is for the first time seen and known.

Here, then, is Hui-neng himself on some of his teaching:

'Learned Audience, the Wisdom of Enlightenment is inherent in every one of us. It is because of the delusion under which our mind works that we fail to realize it ourselves, and that we have to seek the advice and the guidance of enlightened ones before we can know our Essence of Mind. You should know that so far as Buddha-nature is concerned, there is no difference between an enlightened man and an ignorant one. What makes the difference is that one realizes it, while the other is ignorant of it. Now, let me talk to you about Maha Prajnaparamita, so that each of you can attain wisdom.

'Learned Audience, those who recite the word "Prajna" the whole day long do not seem to know that Prajna is inherent in their own nature. But mere talking on food will not appease hunger, and this is exactly the case with these people. We might talk on Sunyata (the Void) for myriads of kalpas, but talking alone will not enable us to realize the Essence of Mind, and it serves no purpose in the end.

'Learned Audience, when you hear me talk about the Void, do not at once fall into the idea of vacuity (because this involves the heresy of the doctrine of annihilation). It is of the utmost importance that we should not fall into this idea, because when a man sits quietly and keeps his mind blank, he will abide in a state of "Voidness of Indifference".

'Learned Audience, the illimitable Void of the universe is capable of holding myriads of things of various shape and form, such as the sun, the moon, stars, mountains, rivers, worlds, springs, rivulets, bushes, woods, good men, bad men, Dharmas pertaining to goodness or badness, Deva planes, hells, great oceans, and all the mountains of the Mahameru. Space takes in all these, and so does the voidness of our nature. We say that the Essence of Mind is great because it embraces all things, since all things are within our nature. When we see the goodness or badness of other people we are not attracted by it, nor repelled by it, nor attached to it; so that our attitude of mind is as void as space.

'Learned Audience, what is Prajna? It means "Wisdom". If at all times and in all places we steadily keep our thought free from foolish desire, and act wisely on all occasions, then we are practising Prajna. One foolish notion is enough to shut off Prajna, while one wise thought will bring it forth again. People in ignorance or under delusion do not see it; they talk about it with their tongues, but in their mind they remain ignorant. They are always saying that they practise Prajna, and they talk incessantly on "Vacuity"; but they do not know the "Absolute Void". "The Heart of Wisdom" is Prajna, which has neither form nor characteristic. If we interpret it in this way, then indeed it is the wisdom of Prajna.

'Prajna does not vary with different persons; what makes the difference is whether one's mind is enlightened or deluded. He who does not know his own Essence of Mind, and is under the delusion that Buddhahood can be attained by outward religious rites is called the slow-witted. He who knows the teaching of the "Sudden" School and attaches no importance to rituals, and whose mind functions always under right views, so that he is absolutely free from defilements or contaminations, is said to have known his Essence of Mind.

'Learned Audience, all Sutras and Scriptures of the Mahayana and Hinayana Schools, as well as the twelve sections of the canonical writings, were provided to suit the different needs and temperaments of various people. It is upon the principle that Prajna is latent in every man that the doctrines expounded in these books are established. If there were no human beings, there would be no Dharmas; hence we know that all Dharmas are made for men, and that all Sutras owe their existence to the preachers. Since some men are wise, the so-called superior men, and some are ignorant, the so-called inferior men, the wise preach to the ignorant when the latter ask them to do so. Through this the ignorant may attain sudden enlightenment, and their mind thereby becomes illuminated. Then they are no longer different from the wise men.'

The inevitability of the 'sudden' moment of enlightenment is brilliantly shown in this brief extract from the Sayings of Shen-hui, one of Hui-neng's most notable disciples:

'Conversion,' said Shen-hui, 'can be either sudden or gradual; both delusion and the Awakening can come to pass slowly or swiftly. That delusion can go on for æon after æon and the Awakening can come in a single moment is an idea that is difficult to understand. I want first to illustrate the point by a comparison; I think it will help you to understand what I mean. A single bundle of thread is made up of innumerable separate strands; but if you join them together into a rope and put it on a plank, you can easily cut through all these threads with one stroke of a sharp knife. Many though the threads may be, they cannot resist that one blade. With those who are converted to the way of the Bodhisattvas, it is just the same. If they meet with a true Good Friend who by skilful means brings them to immediate perception of the Absolute, with Diamond Wisdom they cut through the passions that belong to all the stages of Bodhisattvahood. They suddenly understand and are awakened, and see for themselves that the True Nature of the dharmas is empty and still. Their intelligence is so sharpened and brightened that it can penetrate unimpeded. When this happens to them, all the myriad entanglements of causation are cut away, and erroneous thoughts many as the sands of the Ganges in one moment suddenly cease. Limitless virtues are theirs, ready and complete. The Diamond Wisdom is at work, and failure now impossible.'

Huang-Po (d. 850) lived a century after Hui-neng. His teaching was written down by a contemporary and pupil, so it is only second in value to his own writing. The collection of his sermons number thirty-six. Here is No. 1:

'No. 1. The Master said to me: All the Buddhas and all sentient beings are nothing but the One Mind, beside which nothing exists. This Mind, which is without beginning, is unborn and indestructible. It is not green nor yellow, and has neither form nor appearance. It does not belong to the categories of things which exist or do not exist, nor can it be thought of in terms of new or old. It is neither long nor short, big nor small, for it transcends all limits, measures, names, traces and comparisons. It is that which you see before you – begin to reason about it and you at once fall into error. It is like the boundless void which cannot be fathomed or measured. The One Mind alone is the Buddha, and there is no distinction between the Buddha and sentient things, but that sentient beings are attached to forms and so seek externally for Buddhahood. By their very seeking they lose it, for that is using the Buddha to seek for the Buddha and using mind to grasp Mind. Even though they do their utmost for a full æon, they will not be able to attain to it. They do not know that if they put a stop to conceptual thought and forget their anxiety, the Buddha will appear before them, for this Mind is the Buddha and the Buddha is all living beings. It is not the less for being manifested in ordinary beings, nor is it greater for being manifested in the Buddhas.'

This is clear enough. 'Let the mind abide nowhere', for there is only Mind, and this Mind, which is No-Mind, cannot be caged in any idea nor limited at all. The appearance of two-ness is an illusion which we shall learn to overcome. Only the intuition is in touch with Mind at this level. Develop it, therefore, and keep the thinking mind on a short lead. Use it in the world of duality, but never delude yourself for a single moment into believing that thought alone can *know*.

All this writing speaks of the same experience of the Prajna-paramita – the 'Wisdom that has gone beyond' – as set out in the Mahayana Scriptures of Chapter Six. In brief sermons of pungent dialogue, by words or no words, the great Zen masters pointed, as their Indian predecessors, to the One, and to THAT which lies beyond it; but they taught differently on how to achieve it. Their teaching, being so enigmatic, compressed and irrational, is hard for the Western mind to understand. Here, then, to conclude, is an extract from the glorious poem of the third Chinese Patriarch, Seng-t'san which he called 'On Trust in the Heart'. It may be asked why, as it seems the most simple, it is put at the end of so much harder reading. The answer is that although it is simple it is at the same time enormously profound, and until it is realized that these are not moral maxims for the class-room, but fragments from a vast and deep experience, the quintessence of all the teaching that has gone before, they will not be appreciated at their true value.

ON TRUST IN THE HEART

1. The perfect way knows no difficulties
   Except that it refuses to make preferences;
   Only when freed from hate and love
   It reveals itself fully and without disguise;
   A tenth of an inch's difference,
   And heaven and earth are set apart.
   If you wish to see it before your own eyes
   Have no fixed thoughts either for or against it.

2. To set up what you like against what you dislike –
   That is the disease of the mind:
   When the deep meaning (of the Way) is not understood,
   Peace of mind is disturbed to no purpose.

3. (The Way) is perfect like unto vast space,
   With nothing wanting, nothing superfluous.
   It is indeed due to making choice
   That its Suchness is lost sight of.

4. Pursue not the outer entanglements,
   Dwell not in the inner Void;
   Be serene in the oneness of things,
   And dualism vanishes by itself.

5. When you strive to gain quiescence by stopping motion,
   The quiescence thus gained is ever in motion;
   As long as you tarry in the dualism,
   How can you realize oneness?

6. And when oneness is not thoroughly understood,
   In two ways loss is sustained:
   The denying of reality is the asserting of it,
   And the asserting of emptiness is the denying of it.

7. Wordiness and intellection –
   The more with them, the farther astray we go:
   Away, therefore, with wordiness and intellection,
   And there is no place where we cannot pass freely.

8. When we return to the root, we gain the meaning;
   When we pursue external objects we lose the reason.
   The moment we are enlightened within,
   We go beyond the voidness of a world confronting us.

9. Transformations going on in an empty world which
          confronts us
   Appear real all because of ignorance:
   Try not to seek after the true.
   Only cease to cherish opinions.

In these few stanzas is much of the Mahayana teaching at
its highest level. It is not given as metaphysics, nor as great

abstractions to be brought to earth by the individual mind. The Master is speaking simply and clearly; he means what he says, and he says precisely what he means. What he says applies to East and West, to North and South, at all times and in all places. And this includes the West today.

CHAPTER TWELVE

ZEN COMES WEST

THIS is a statement of fact, and it has many meanings. First, Zen is, of course, but a name for an experience as old as history. Meister Eckhart, perhaps the greatest European mystic, was clearly an enlightened man, in the sense that he had a 'major' experience of satori. The same may be said of other mystics, while numberless writers, in prose and poetry, have shown their 'minor' awakenings. R. H. Blyth has collected scores of these in his *Zen in English Literature,* and any lover of poetry will find many more.

But Zen as such came West many years ago. Until the publication of Dr. D. T. Suzuki's three volumes of *Essays in Zen Buddhism,* beginning in 1927, we knew very little of Zen Buddhism, and nothing of the Zen at the heart of it. But now for sixty years this greatest Buddhist scholar of the century has been teaching the English-speaking world the essentials of Zen Buddhism, not only as an expert in Chinese and Japanese religious history, but as an enlightened man. He clearly knew his destiny at an early age, and on hearing in 1897 that he was offered a post with a Buddhist publisher in Chicago, he intensified his work under his Roshi, and in the ten months left to him before this departure, he 'got it'. Since then he has taught in two capacities, to fellow scholars as an expert in his subject; but to those who sought the way of Zen and the goal of it, as a Master speaking from the plane of his enlightenment.

His major works in English now number eighteen, and I have a collection of a dozen more in Japanese awaiting his translation. When the history of Zen Buddhism in the West comes to be written, none will doubt that its coming is to the credit of one man, Daisetz Teitaro Suzuki. To date no Western writer on Zen has been uninfluenced by his writing, and all the early writers, including Alan Watts, Dr. Benoit of Paris, and myself, derived the greater part of our knowledge from his pen.

A few obtained their knowledge from other sources; Eugen Herrigel from his Japanese archery instructor, Trevor Leggett from the field of Judo, Ruth Sasaki from her late husband, Sokei-an Sasaki, a Rinzai Zen Roshi, while the late Nyogen Senzaki of California was a contemporary of Dr. Suzuki's at Engakuji. Mr. Robert Linssen, the leader of a group in Brussels, has woven together the threads of Zen Buddhism and Krishnamurti; 'Wei Wu Wei', an Irishman living on the Continent, has used his brilliant brain to study the writings of the masters themselves, on the reasonable assumption that they meant what they said; and that what they said is more important than all the commentaries written or to come.

And now we have the 'Scriptures' of Zen, that is, the writings used in Zen monasteries; the collections of Mondo, and the sermons of three or four of the great masters, as recorded by their pupils. Ch'an Buddhism, in the sense of the Chinese tradition as distinct from that which came through Japan, has entered the field with Chang Chen-Chi's *The Practice of Zen* and Charles Luk's translations called *Ch'an and Zen Teaching*. Soto Zen, the twin of Rinzai Zen, which also came from China to Japan in the twelfth to thirteenth century, is still very little understood, and we have but two short works on the subject to inform us. It will be interesting to see what happens when a sufficiency of books on this aspect of Zen is available to the Western seeker of Zen enlightenment. Which school will be the more popular, and why?

So much for history, for works on Zen, good, not so good and offensively untrue are now coming onto the bookstalls fast, too fast for our wise consumption. What is the West's reaction to all this material? To answer this we must generalize on the Western mind. As compared with that of China and

Japan it is intellectual, extravert and 'scientific'. Herein lies an enormous difficulty and some hope. The difficulty is in accepting the very existence of a faculty in the human mind which is higher than thought. The strength of the West is in its intellect; science in all its forms, such as technology; all forms of automation; the 'modern' approach to farming, medicine and to religion itself; even the mind's own science, psychology, all these are the outcome of reasoning, and logic is still the Western yardstick of truth. When, therefore, a new school of Buddhism was brought into its field of inquiry, it was immediately accepted as another 'school of thought' and so examined. The fact that writers on Zen, as the masters themselves, point out that the experience at the heart of Zen is beyond duality, and therefore beyond the range and reach of even the highest thinking, matters not. This new thing had to be examined, and examined with the usual instruments. The 'few', whether we call them natural mystics, or those in whose make-up the god of Reason was never so surely throned, accepted Zen for what it is, a method of training for the development of a faculty higher than the intellect whereby to break through into a new world, not of thought but of Truth itself. They shouted with glee and they are still shouting; the heavy intellectuals are still dissecting Zen in the laboratory and solemnly reporting that there is nothing in it. How nearly right they are! If they could but see that Zen is what it is because there is Nothing – No-thing – in it, they would make a great discovery. Meanwhile it is left to poets, mystics, unspoilt minds and those with a vast sense of humour to see that Zen is Zen because it has left the intellect behind.

So much for the difficulty in a Western acceptance of Zen. Yet the English, like the Chinese, are essentially down-to-earth and practical. They understand work, the satisfaction of a thing well wrought. They are natural craftsmen. When a new idea is presented they ask at once, 'How does it work?' And in order to get an answer they add, 'What do I do?' They are action-minded; so is Zen. 'When hungry eat, when tired sleep.' That is plain enough. As for Saviours, abstract speculations on the Origin of the Universe, and instruments to calculate precisely the moment when a collection of human beings launches an instrument to blow up another collection of human beings – 'Get on with your tea', says the master. He might add, 'Look at the tea-leaves in the cup, not to tell fortunes but to see what they are – what they truly, simply, utterly and absolutely *are*. If you can see what makes a tea-leaf a tea-leaf you know what makes the manifested universe what it is, you know the Suchness of all things and each of them; you are enlightened. So get on with your tea! This appeals to the Western man who is naturally action-minded. He suspects and faintly dislikes the supremely intellectual mind; he is never comfortable with too much cleverness. And as for Bhakti Yoga, the way of devotion, it is not for him, though it is often the natural way for his wife.

Here, then, we have the Western mind, or a few examples of the less thought-ridden of it, facing the Japanese School of Zen. The reader of this work, having patiently come so far, is one of the few. I am another. What are we to do?

We can do one of two things, or find a compromise between them. The student can go to Japan and study there for a substantial period in a Zen monastery; or a qualified Zen master can come to Europe and teach here; or there may be a workable blend of the two. All have their difficulties. As to the first, very few Westerners have the necessary qualifications to go to Japan. The cost is considerable; the time spent in Japan must be at least two to three years, and they are few who have no commitments or duties left to perform, and are free for such a journey. The student must learn Japanese, and though much may be learnt before leaving home, this involves preparing for the enterprise for one or two years in advance. Health has to be considered; the average European does not take kindly to Japanese diet, either as to its quantity or quality. Next, age is a factor, for to learn to sit cross-legged in the 'lotus' posture is difficult indeed in middle-age.

And there must be sufficient background of education, and sufficient intelligence to think, before the student can usefully attempt to go further than the strongest thought can reach. And finally, the new seeker of Zen must satisfy the Roshi that he has the 'great spirit of inquiry', the sheer strength of will, necessary to break through into Reality.

The visitor to Japan, therefore, will always be rare. What of the reverse process? Two things are needed, a Roshi who speaks good English and is at the same time willing to come.

But first, who wants him, and how badly? Nearly all who would benefit by his training are either working during the day or otherwise occupied. This means that the Roshi's use to the students would be in the evening only, with additional classes at week-ends. What would he do all day? And how many of those who attend a class would be able to do so four or five nights a week? For the claims of duty are paramount. No man has the right for his own spiritual advantage to abandon existing claims and duties. He must earn his freedom from such ties, and then make use of it. The group who would learn from the master's teaching would therefore be small. And in which city is the Roshi to live, when such students, few in number, are scattered over the face of Europe? The whole point of the Roshi's presence is the regular meeting of the student face to face with the teacher. How, if the master lives in Europe, but five hundred miles away?

Let us look at precedent, for there is one in New York. For many years the First Zen Institute of New York worked for the advent of a Roshi. Its members sat in meditation four or five nights a week, for long hours, practising the Zen form of watching the breath – nothing more. Then a Roshi came, on a visit, and after a while went away. Then he came again on a longer visit, and went away. Finally, having gained a fair knowledge of English he has, at the time of writing, come to stay. But his pupils are still but a score or so, and this is for New York only. Let us suppose that such a Roshi, able to teach in the West, and willing to come, were persuaded that he could better spend his time with a handful of Western students than teaching in Japan, we repeat that he would but serve the students of one city, or perhaps one or more cities on a circuit not too large. And those who sat at his feet would have to pay for his keep.

So the problem is a real one, and it is not enough to quote the profoundly true and ancient statement, 'When the pupil is ready, the Master appears.' For this implies that the pupil in question is far advanced by his own efforts, and now needs, and has earned, the physical presence of a master.

This raised the question – How many at any one time and in any one place have reached the point where the Roshi is not wasting his time upon them? The master musician does not teach the very rudiments of his instrument to children, and the man who aims at the summit of Everest does not trouble the master-climber until he has learned the elements of climbing and considerable muscle-control. In other words, what right have we to a Roshi? At present, what spiritual need? Surely we must at first submit to the order, 'Teach yourself', and practise it a long way. We must read and study and meditate on basic principles. We must learn to know ourselves, and humbly consider what men have learned already in the field of spiritual endeavour, before attempting ourselves to achieve.

It may be that we have to admit a clear distinction between two stages of spiritual progress; our own path to the entrance to the one Path, and the treading of that Path itself. How else do we reconcile the two great statements, 'The ways to the One are as many as the lives of men', and 'Thou canst not tread the Path before thou has become that Path thyself'? Surely the Path is one, but it may be a long while before the would-be treader of it reaches the entrance. Is not this entrance the gate of 'conversion', of the Bodhisattva Vow, of the spiritual 'point of no return'? And are we not stumbling blindly through the gloom of our own ignorance to find that gate? Initiation into the mysteries of the Way needs no divine

Initiator save as we choose to project that concept out of the human mind. We test ourselves, or are tested by our own past karma; we succeed in or we fail that test – and it may be that we shall fail it again and again. Then suddenly, yes, suddenly, we are on the Way, and thereafter there is but one command, Walk on! – and one obedience.

This is most pertinent to our inquiry. Is there one Zen training, for all men, everywhere? Perhaps, in the sense of the final stages, but may there not be a thousand ways of approaching the point where that final training begins?

This raises the highly contentious problem of 'square Zen' and 'beat Zen', and it cannot be thrust aside. Does Zen training, *for our purposes, here and now*, mean that which is to be found in a Japanese Zen monastery, or will the West create its own, or a dozen versions of its own – as good? Surely the suggested distinction between paths to the Path and the Path itself may provide the answer. The student can go a long way, perhaps a very long way, on his own path to the Gate, which is the 'Gateless Gate' of Zen Buddhism. Only there will he need, and therefore find, the Master who can guide him further.

Alan Watts has written wisely on the problem of 'Square', that is to say, traditional Zen training, and 'Beat', or the modern American version which, for all its brash impertinence, has a spiritual core. In *This is It* he talks of frames and their limitation. We need a frame in which to see any situation, in which to use it, and fifteen hundred years of the Zen School have built an elaborate and strongly-moulded frame for Zen training. But a frame can kill the life of the situation by too rigid limitation. Thus, however good a form of government, or education, or art, in the end the life which created it kills it. Our bodies die from too much life, not from too little; it is the one Life which, as the body or mould grows hard, breaks it with the force of life, and life moves on into other forms. So the Zen tradition of Japan, though still right for the Japanese, may not be right, and even be wrong for the

West to imitate. As Watts points out, there is no real 'way' to Satori, 'so the way you are following makes very little difference.' Nevertheless I hold that one must tread some way, or way to the one Way, and a method that has worked successfully for a very long time is not lightly to be cast aside.

For Beat Zen is not a true alternative; rather it is an exaggeration of a truth, a truth and a half as someone said, which is as bad as a half-truth. Life should be spontaneous, unbound by the rules, ideals and even the values of those about one. But this does not mean that 'anything goes', that morality and social conventions of right behaviour are all to be broken and flung aside for the sake of breaking them. It is a spiritual paradox that there is only freedom in control, and the personality presented to the world must be controlled from within if the mind is to be free for its own development.

Applying this to the problem in hand, there must be some training, but it must be an inward process applied by the individual to his own mind. Even the Roshi does not behave like a hooligan. His outer life is largely conventional; his mind, set free from limitation by his enlightenment, can use convention while being no longer bound by it.

In the West, then, we need not import entire the Zen training of Japan. At the same time, learning from its long experience, we must devise a method of our own. What shall it be? In New York the students seem to have assumed that there was nothing to be done before a Roshi arrived save to practise Zen sitting while meditating on the breath. I do not accept this view. I am satisfied, after twenty years' experience, that much may be done, both negatively and positively, to prepare the mind for the advanced help of a Roshi, and that the qualities derived from Za-zen alone are not sufficient nor even the most important. I believe that one must start at a deeper level of the self, to clear the foundations before one attempts to build. I agree with Alan Watts, that the Westerner attracted by Zen 'must understand his own culture so thoroughly that he is no longer swayed by its premises unconsciously. He must really have come to terms with the Lord God Jehovah and with his Hebrew-Christian conscience so that he can take it or leave it without fear or rebellion. He must be free of the itch to justify himself. For Zen is above all the liberation of the mind from conventional thought, and this is something utterly different from rebellion against convention, on the one hand, or adopting foreign conventions on the other.'

I was middle-aged before I rid myself of the God-concept, in the sense of a Power outside my own mind which could reward or punish me, and all of us in the West are troubled with that itch to interfere in the lives of others, to put right what we consider wrong, and generally to interfere in the self-governance of the universe. We find it hard to *accept* any situation of which we do not wholly *approve,* and we hold that anything to be done properly must be done according to a predetermined plan which is the 'right' way of doing it – and *we* know what is the right way. All this makes an approach to Zen impossible. Zen IS; it is the Universe itself, and THAT which makes it tick. We must therefore accept it as such, and its Suchness, which, though the indwelling essence of every thing, is itself no-thing, Nothing, Void. We shall grow, therefore, in our training, by growing less. We shall not, as we know ourselves with a name and address, become more important in our neighbours' eyes; we shall grow less, until, content to be 'pushed around' or even ignored, we melt back into the situation's scenery. There we may well remain unnoticed, exhibiting 'nothing special' for our neighbour's praise, but understanding, feeling one with all events and things and people, and helping each as occasion permits, without fuss or bother, without planned purpose or the least thought of reward. For the Zen ideal is not the normal ideal of the holy man. The Roshi himself may look like and indeed live like a tramp, as many of the Chinese masters of old, but his 'great compassionate heart' will be ever alive to helping a fellow form of life, however great or small, according to its need.

How many Western students can face this new ideal, and genuinely adopt it? How many look for a system of self-training which is designed to help them to get rid of self? Let us look at the man that we ought to want to be.

Freed from attachment to the background of his heredity, education, and social environment, with its sense of values based on the growth of 'self', he will live henceforth in 'Now', forgetful of the past and careless of the future, free of regrets and hopes and fears. Thus 'sitting loose to life', avoiding opinions, views, conclusions and indeed all binding concepts as a bird avoids the bird-lime spread for it in a tree, he seeks for no security, accepts with equal indifference pleasure and pain, and knows, as he 'walks on' and 'walks on' without ceasing, that 'It's all right', and there is nothing wrong anywhere.

This for the Westerner is difficult indeed. We are driven into foolish karma-producing action by our sense of conscience, which is a sense of guilt. Who put it there? Someone did, for it is not natural, and that which is unnatural has no place in Zen. Do we really need such a nagging voice within, to poison all our pleasure and the heart's delight? If not, let us quietly drop it; but it all takes time!

Says *The Voice of the Silence*, 'The Path is one for all; the means to reach the goal must vary with the pilgrims'. Let us examine these means, and provide ideas for the formulation of our own.

CHAPTER THIRTEEN

TRAINING FOR ZEN - I

WE are now in a position to consider the actual process of self-training towards the Zen experience. But why so late, in a book which purports to treat of self-training for Zen? There are several answers. The first is, that just as a builder must first clear the site on which to build, so the Western mind must study and partially break free from the complex of thought and values inherent in his religious and cultural background. Consciously or subconsciously this background has a theist bias, whether as Christian or Jew. There is the thought, however faded, of a Saviour-God who will, at a price, lead a soul worth saving from earth to Heaven, from death to Immortality. Priests have their part in this, and ritual. Morality is a code of conduct to be disobeyed at peril, and the whole process of this religious life is felt to be scarcely compatible with science and psychology. The Zen life springs from concepts and values so utterly different from these that Western minds of the highest calibre have doubted whether Zen development can proceed from such a starting point. For the mental background of a child born into a Zen family is still profoundly different. It knows no God, no Saviour, no priest to serve this God, and no salvation in some Heaven. It knows no self save the unimportant personality, doomed to fade out rapidly as development moves on, yet it knows of a 'Buddha within' or 'Essence of Mind' which is 'intrinsically pure', and needs no saving. So far from binding itself in a cocoon of conventional morality, the cultured Eastern mind is ready to drop all rules and laws whatever in acquiring a new spontaneity of action. 'Let the mind abide nowhere' replaces the Western ideal of a set of 'sound principles' of what it is right to believe and do, which can be referred to and applied in each and every circumstance, social, moral and political. And behind the conscious mind of the West is the 'unconscious' of Western psychology, while behind the Eastern mentality is some awareness of the Zen Unconscious, the Void or Suchness of things, the 'Store-consciousness' of the Mind-only school, or some other variant on the Buddha-nature which is the heart of the Cosmos and of every 'thing' within it.

A second answer to the question which opened this chapter will now be obvious, that all that has preceded it, if well digested and applied, will have prepared the mind of the reader for this profound and lasting change. I have long regarded principles as forces in the mind. What container would remain the same if the Niagara Falls were poured into it? Yet principles such as Karma, Karuna and Sunyata are each of a power commensurate, and must, if genuinely accepted, profoundly change the mind that bravely takes them in. The doctrine of change, for example, is a tremendous force, for it sweeps away in its flood all thoughts of security, insurance, settling down or other forms of 'stopping'. The doctrine of Karma, cause/effect, gives meaning to each smallest act but kills all thought of projected blame, or hope of good luck or fortune. Suffering must now be borne, not feared. We caused it, and it will go so soon as we remove its cause and not before. If Life is one then men are brothers, and should live accordingly. If Prajna/Karuna are quite inseverable twins, then Wisdom is not worth acquiring unless each moment it is applied in acts of Compassion, nor Compassion helpful unless directed by the Wisdom which knows what to do. If Truth in fact lies utterly beyond the intellect, then we must develop forthwith whatever faculty we need to find Truth on its own plane. If Nirvana truly *is* Samsara, the Light itself already within each lamp of circumstance, then away with Heaven as a condition of some other place and time; Hell is here too, as we suffer from our sins, not for them. And we now know the Way which leads to the right use of these forces, by a Mind now one with them. Only concentration and years of meditation will expand our present limited instruments to their true dimensions; meanwhile we shall not fear to enter the world of paradox and silence in which that developed understanding needs must dwell.

There is yet another answer to that question. Before the training begins the would-be trainee must have built up what a London student calls 'a spiritual head of steam'. Whether or not Zen training as here described will actually produce the 'moment' of satori, an enormous concentration of force is needed for the break-through, and considerable pressure is needed even to begin the training with any likelihood of success. And the long, slow study and assimilation of doctrine is one stage of such development. Then 'suddenly' the tension is released in a 'moment' of vision, and the needed power is transmuted for a while into so much Light, if that analogy be useful, only to be built up for the next assault on the barriers we have so long maintained against our own enlightenment.

Is Training Possible?

It may seem late to raise this doubt, but it was raised by Hubert Benoit in *The Supreme Doctrine*, and the question must be answered. Satori, he says, is like jumping a ditch, and no training can do more than bring one to the edge of the ditch. What then remains is the existential jump from Duality into Non-duality. But, as he points out, 'no amelioration of something imperfect will ever reach perfection.' The perfect man, in the sense of the very wise or very saintly man, is in a sense no nearer Satori than he was in his imperfection, for the direction to be taken for Satori is, as it were, at right angles to perfection as we conceive it. Self-discipline, he argues, or Zen training in this sense, puts the aspiring mind in blinkers, even in a strait-jacket, and the Zen mind must be free. But here is a profound paradox, that only in self-imposed limitation are we truly free. Beginning with particular discipline we move to the ideal of no discipline, which is the greatest form of it, for here 'the mind abides nowhere', we 'cease to cherish opinions' and while using concepts we are bound by none of them. The very spontaneity of action which is the ideal of Zen, as of Taoism, is only attained by a system of training which is as ruled and fettered as the resulting condition of mind is divinely free. Only in persistent and pitiless negation, in doctrine and in self-control, shall we reach the supreme affirmation – Yes! It is Good, it is All Right!

We face, then, another paradox, what Dr. Evola has called 'cultivation through non-cultivation', to do what is next to be done with no deliberate mind, without motive or thought of result. Only thus shall we prepare ourselves, in the mystical sense as a vessel pure enough to receive Grace, in the physical sense as a runner who, in preparation for the supreme achievement, trains his every muscle to that end. The preparation will not *cause* Satori; let that be clearly seen. But it provides the conditions in which the major experience is at least most likely to arrive.

I hold, therefore, on the strength of reasoning and long experience, my own and that of others, that Zen training, in the sense here used, is worth the effort from the viewpoint of Zen, and utterly worth the effort in the expansion of those qualities we look for in great character, and which together form the ideal of a noble mind.

Seven Questions to be Answered

I believe that every would-be student of Zen should be able to answer seven questions, at least to himself. And I believe that an utterly true answer shows much progress up the hillside of Zen training.

What is it you want?

Do you know? If the answer is Satori, what do you believe it to be? Is a search of use if you know not what you are seeking? If the answer, from the deeps of mind, is that you seek for nothing, and find no need for the carrot on the donkey's nose, that is evidence of a developing intuition, by which, we are agreed, the experience can alone arrive.

But is it *true* that in your search you have passed the point of needing to know what you are seeking? Is it true? If not, ask yourself again, what do you want?

Why do you want it?

Motive is of increasing importance as the chosen path moves straight uphill. The purpose, or at least the result of true Zen training is to reduce the value of self to vanishing point. It is therefore useless to train for Zen if the secret purpose of the training is to magnify the self being trained. It is another paradox, and a shock to many a Western mind, to find that in Zen a man grows steadily less in the eyes of his fellow men, not more. He is quite content to be 'pushed around' by his fellows, seeks no seat of power, nor praise nor gratitude. In some religions the Holy Man is a figure of adoration and renown. But many of the greatest of Zen Masters of the past behaved and looked like tramps, and were regarded as mildly mad. Only the few, with an opened eye of Buddhi, saw the greatness within the utterly happy but apparently irresponsible life of the sage. Motive, then, is vital, for this and for another reason, that as we grow in spiritual stature the motive force of every act should be the welfare of mankind. Only when the Bodhisattva Vow, to work for all mankind 'until the last blade of grass is entered into Buddhahood', is working deeply in the mind is the final motive for each action ready to be born, no motive, 'purposelessness'. This is beyond most of us now, yet some of our finest actions are of this quality.

How much do you want it?

How much are you prepared to pay for what you want? In effort, perpetual concentration on the job in hand, 'mindful' at each moment of the day? In time, for the necessary study, deep study, of great writings and new points of view, and the regular, utterly regular and increasing periods of meditation? In money, if for you time is money, and you cannot make so much if you spend more time on Zen? In self – the hardest price of all? What 'pleasures' are you prepared to give up, to gain more time for study and for working for other people? What suffering are you now prepared to accept and endure, instead of running away from it in distractions of all kinds? Yet self is the ultimate price to pay for the vision of non-self, which is the Self of Enlightenment. Self is the sacrifice to lay on the altar of Zen, and silently. Are you ready to make it? This does not mean the abnegation of present responsibilities. These must be fulfilled. But for the rest? An utterly honest answer is apt to be frightening.

What wants it?

You say that *you* do, but who are you? In the ideal there is, as Dr. Suzuki points out, no subject that experiences and no object that is experienced, but we are yet far from the ideal. We have, as we now know, a conscious and an unconscious mind, and these are but facets of the manifest mind as distinct from the Zen Unconscious, which to us is No-Mind. Who is it that wants, the lower, desireful mind, full of 'hatred, lust and illusion', or the nobler Self that must, as the Dhammapada says, learn to be 'lord of self'? Some measure of self-analysis is helpful, to let us see what a perambulating civil war we take about with us, of hostile and discordant elements pulling and pushing in utterly different directions. At least we may learn to recognize our basic type in Jungian terms. The emotional introvert and the intellectual extrovert will find it hard to agree on spiritual policy. The intuitive, who may be intellectual or emotional, intro- or extro-vert, will seldom have patience with the cold-blooded intellectual. And so on. Even astrology can help here, for the classification of character, apart from vulgar 'fortune-telling' can be remarkably accurate and helpful.

Where are your looking for it?

The answer should be easy, but is it honest? Of course the answer is in the first place 'within', but are you truly searching within, or have you a lingering hope that some God or Teacher or marvellous book will save you the trouble of long years of spiritual development? And is 'within' the final answer? Not in Zen, where there is no within or without, and Samsara *is* Nirvana, and Enlightenment only to be found in humble, daily things. 'There is nothing infinite,' says Dr. Suzuki, 'apart from finite things.' Do we live accordingly?

Have you the guts to find it?

Use, if you will, a more delicate term. Call it a compound of courage, will-power and endurance, but it is what we commonly know as 'guts', and we shall need a great deal of it. Psychologists say that the will is powerful in proportion as it is geared to 'affects', the modern name for emotion. If this is anaemic, so is the will. This is profoundly important, for it shows the value of what I have long described as 'spiritual excitement'. Dr Suzuki, in *Living by Zen* speaks of the necessary shocks which the mind needs to assist it to break through to Reality, and the power for this may come from 'intense emotional excitement', whether the emotion be high or low. At its highest I believe it to be an emotional reaction to a mind, in the sense of the thinking mind, suddenly illumined with the Light of truth through the developing faculty of the intuition. The placid mind, not to be confused with the truly serene mind, gets nowhere. A sudden flash of Truth is profoundly exciting, and I know no better term for the experience. But guts are needed to work up this 'head of steam', tremendous will-power applied to a chosen end, without let-up or the least pause on the way.

For the difficulties to be overcome are great in quantity and size, and none the less so for being largely the product of the very force that works to enlightenment. We create the resistance, as we build up the power of a pendulum to swing back at us by the power with which we push it away. Mental calm, if we ever had it, will disappear before storms of doubt and despair. There will be psychic eruptions, embarrassing, disgusting, frightening, all of which must be calmly met, faced for what they are, and allowed to disperse. And there will be upsurges from our own and the racial unconscious, mostly unpleasant to the current state of mind.

Are you fit for the journey?

It must be clearly understood that Zen is no form of psycho-analysis, in the sense of treatment for a weak or unbalanced mind. The psychiatrist is treating a sick mind; the Zen student starts with a whole one, or at least a reasonably well-balanced one, which needs but assistance in finding its own indwelling Enlightenment.

Three More Questions

Three more questions, and we can at last begin. Do you realize that the training is all and every day? There is no such thing as a time for Zen; there are twenty-four hours out of every twenty-four. Zen is a way of living life; more accurately, living life as life lives itself. It is not a hobby for the casual moment or the wet week-end; nor a new study, as a foreign language or even mind-control. It is a work for the total man in every time and place and in all that he totally does.

But it lies beyond thinking, and the uttermost reach of thought. Is that *truly* understood? We must ask ourselves this question again and again. I know of students who for years have striven mightily to find enlightenment, but because they seek it in thought they will never find. The greater the intellect the harder this fact to learn. Zen is born where thought falls dying, and hands the torch of effort to the faculty which alone can know, the intuition. Zen cannot be proved; it knows no measurement. It is no 'thing', and is therefore for ever beyond the realm of science. The head thinks; the heart feels, and it is the heart that knows.

Meanwhile the search is unceasing, and the first findings will be unpleasant. Is that realized now, so that it does not form a fog of bewilderment and disillusion later on the way? All deliberate effort brings down an avalanche of karmic consequences, great or small. And the step from cosmos to chaos is always unsettling, and sometimes frightening. Our lives are based on what is reasonable and common sense; truth is apt to be neither. From a well-worn path we step into a fog wherein lie precipices, quagmires and a howling wilderness. We must learn to walk on, through nonsense to a noble Non-sense, from the tramlines of a settled mind, through the trackless desert of no meaning, to the freedom of a 'mind that alights nowhere', and is based for ever on No-thought, No-purpose and No-difference of any kind.

Is all this understood? At least in principle? Then let us begin. But you have begun; indeed you are well on the Way! For the hardest step is the first. He who begins has but to continue, and in this as in so much else the first and the last rule for achievement is: Begin, and then – go on! At first you will be consciously driving yourself forward; then you will be unhappy without a day of Zen. Finally, Zen will be driving you from within, to an ever-increasing power of Prajna, Wisdom, expressing itself unceasingly in Karuna, Compassion for all that lives.

CHAPTER FOURTEEN

TRAINING FOR ZEN - II

HERE, then, are some notes for the actual self-training. All have been better written elsewhere, by Dr. Suzuki with a wealth of illustration from the masters of old, and by Westerners who have sought to make these points, as I have made them yet again for another audience. Many of them, indeed, have appeared more than once in this present volume. Yet repetition is needed, and still more repetition, if the heavy furniture of past opinion is to be thrust aside, and the light of No-Mind be allowed to circulate in a mind set free. By whomsoever given they are but hints, for more cannot be given. A master can teach his pupil how to sit, how to keep still, how to learn control of mind by counting the breaths. The rest is a path which must be laid down by the pupil before he can tread it; thereafter, however encouraged, he walks alone. But these themes or principles are tremendous powers in the mind. Let each be taken in meditation daily for a single month and much will happen! They are as ferment in the mind or, as some say, dynamite. None can use them in meditation and remain unaffected. If you doubt this statement, try!

Experience Only

Henceforward nothing matters save experience. Buddhism is only a collection of thought and doctrine about the Buddha's Enlightenment. But the words about it matter not; no Scripture will take the mind one foot upon the Way. Zen is not a system of philosophy, nor of psychology, nor of meditation, and when it tries to explain itself in these terms it ceases to be Zen. The Buddhist Scriptures, and the Zen equivalent, are records of so many men's achievement, a description of their experience. Their use to us, if any, is to stimulate our minds to the like experience, and Buddhism is only of value as it serves to train its students to that end. For the like reason, Zen is concerned with experience and not with its modes of expression. It matters not what the student says to the master if it shows the experience to be genuine, nor how profound a new book about Zen, how brilliant, if it is not based on direct awareness of the Zen described.

In Zen the means is the end; the end and the means are one. To find true Suchness in the job in hand is utterly sufficient. Once found, and the world is never the same again to the eyes that have seen. Test, then, every utterance and written word of one who speaks of Zen. Is it still 'about it and about', or has it the flavour of Prajna, Wisdom? Does the speaker speak 'as one having authority, and not as the Scribes', as was said of Jesus? This is the test of experience, or high or low, that the writer or speaker clearly *knows*: this is the true test of all writing alleged to be Scriptural. In Zen there is no authority for any man save his own experience, nor respect for a teacher save that he tries to assist his pupil to achieve his own. The intellect will reason to its own approval, and may clearly prove that Zen does not exist; the heart knows otherwise, and the 'soul' or 'higher Self', whatever that may be, is silent, knowing what it knows.

The Intuition

What, then, is the intuition, and how do we develop it? Dr. Suzuki, speaking of the work of the Zen master, once said that 'the insight he has gained into Reality must be organized into a system of intuitions so that it will grow richer in content. The insight itself is contentless, for to be so is its very condition.' But he goes on to say that this emptiness is no abstraction, but a dynamic force which motivates all other aspects of the Buddhist life. Each aspect of the training should be ruled from the intuition, for all of it is designed to its development. Assume its existence, and then use it. Trust its whispering, its sudden flashes of an understanding which the reason may not follow at that time. If in my earlier *Zen Buddhism* I said any more on developing the intuition, it amounts to no more than this. Once the faculty is known to exist it will shine the more in the darkness of our reasoning. Said the Egyptian Hierophants of old, 'The Light is within thee; let the Light shine!'

'Seeing directly into the heart of man'

This famous line in the summary of Zen attributed to Bodhidharma, the founder of the School of Zen, can form the basis of a volume of commentary, and a few notes here may help. The first word is to 'see', and seeing has a meaning of its own in Zen. The artist is trained to see things as they are, which means that he must look at them, hard and long and without reaction. In the same way a Zen student learns to look at things, hard and long, but he finds that they are not as the artist sees them. Hence the Chinese saying: In the beginning, mountains are seen as mountains and trees as trees. With a little progress mountains are no longer mountains and trees no longer trees. But with enlightenment, mountains are once more seen as mountains and trees as trees.' First, then, we accept things as they seem to be. Then we find they are not so, and we analyse them into their ever-changing and unreal constituents. We learn to accept them as what they now seem to be, the actor without his mask, the situation stripped of its glamour, the laws of our being whether we approve of them or not. We begin to break up large and abstract concepts, and see their danger to the evolving mind. What is this thing called the State, what is Peace, what, indeed, is Reality? We do not know, and 'define' them merely by a further batch of concepts. So we learn to be less fooled by others' opinions, slogans, clichés, and ignorant, one-sided views. We begin to think for ourselves, and increasingly to form no opinions or views. We learn to distinguish our own reactions of like/dislike from our decisions on true/untrue, and to distrust all of them. We feel less fear, of the dentist or the 'future'; we hope less, that it will keep fine or that 'it will be all right'; we care less, whether we succeed or fail, are thanked or not, or even noticed. Situations are more coolly appraised. The eye sees now more deeply into the causing of all situations, and the almost inevitable effect of others' (and our own) persistent folly. The heart of compassion sees what can be done, or cannot, but helps to the hilt wherever a fellow form of life has need. We learn to blame less, to take the responsibility for our own condition. As Epictetus, the Stoic slave remarked, 'If any man be unhappy, let him know that it is by reason of himself alone.'

With deeper and deeper seeing we detach ourselves from things and situations, while entering them according to the moment's need. We can enter a mould without being caged in it, obey the laws and moral rules of our society without being bound by them. 'Do what you will,' as someone said, 'but not because you must.' We obey to be free by our obedience.

Such seeing leads in time to Zen seeing. 'Seeing is experiencing, seeing things in their state of suchness or is-ness. Buddha's whole philosophy comes from this "seeing".' And this, as Dr. Suzuki says elsewhere, is Blake's 'to hold infinity in the palm of the hand and eternity in an hour'. Then the part is more than the whole; it *is* the whole, and the universe is seen in a grain of sand. Thus did the Buddha see, and in the utmost depths of seeing all things as they are, attain Enlightenment.

Only the final step remains, and we shall take it when the moment comes; to become what we see, to pour the heart and mind into the thing, the situation, until no seer and seen remains – only seeing. Now is the moment of Kensho, the first Zen 'seeing', the prelude to Satori, the essential Zen experience. Now do you see?

Directly

'That which is to be done, let it be done.' Just like that. It sounds simple, but few of us are capable of direct action, of thought or feeling, for one long day. Yet Zen lives in facts and hates abstractions, generalizations, vague opinions. Distinctions, conclusions, codes and fashions, though having their place in the daily round, are not its concern. The man of Zen is precise in feeling, thought and action. He knows what he knows, believes what he believes until that belief is modified, and forms no opinions which it does not seem his duty to form. He shows remarkable economy of effort in action, for he knows what he is doing, and if need be why and how, and he does it. Just like that. Then he moves to the next thing to be done. As the Zen Master Ummon said, 'If you walk, just walk; if you sit, just sit. But don't wobble.'

Absorbed in his actions, large or small, the actor is one with his act. Our senses act directly; why not the man as a whole? A hand in the fire is burnt; we yell, and then attend to the burn. In the same way, said a master, 'When hungry we eat; when tired we sleep.' What is difficult about that? Surely he who sees things as they are can learn to accept them as they are; he needs no shield to hide from him what he sees. But how many of us can face the naked Truth we claim to seek? It was Jung who described religion itself as used by men to shield them from Reality, and many of us run both fast and far to escape it. How much effort is spent in avoiding time to think, and in particular to face ourselves? The stronger of us plunge into so-called pleasure, hobbies, travel, literature; the weak among us into crime, illness, suicide. And all in vain, for sooner or later, in this life or the next, we have to face ourselves, to begin the journey – home. And in modern life even our escape techniques are becoming second-hand. We play our games on television, make our music in a machine, entertain ourselves no longer but use an instrument at second-hand. Our food is no longer fresh, our emotions are stimulated and fed by the cinema and press; our thoughts are very seldom our own. Thus buttressed, by insurance, pensions, regulations, few of us dare 'sit loose to life', dwell happily in insecurity, be naked to experience. We seek Utopias, talk glibly of peace on earth while blaming everyone else for breaking it, set up ideals for others to make true. All will be well, we hope, in some other place, in earth or heaven, at some other time. But what of the here and now, and the job to be done in it? What else shall we ever have to do, but the job in hand, which is here, and now? The casual/precise, efficient yet informal, calm yet utterly direct approach to each situation, such is the Zen way. But how hard to be simple yet immediate and direct? We must try.

The Heart of Man

We know of the personality, the mask through which the true man speaks. This ego, the 'shadow' of Jungian psychology, must sooner or later be 'vomited up' as a Zen teacher put it, and this moment will come when the hour is ripe. Deeper than this is the 'I' that wars with it, the Self that is 'lord of self', mentioned in the *Dhammapada*. Yet both these aspects of the self are in duality; neither is the 'true man' of Zen. Beyond both appearance and reality is Truth, for these are but concepts, names for the two poles of the Unborn, Uncreated when it appears in manifestation. Beyond self and Self is the Essence of Mind, as Hui-neng called it, our 'original Face before our parents were born', the principle of Enlightenment which, when it enters Nirvana, is but returning home. Yet the One has no parts; each part *is* the Whole, and hence 'the Buddha within' of cosmic consciousness. This is the 'Self beyond Self' which in Western terms absorbs both the conscious and the unconscious mind. It is the metaphysical Unconscious of Eastern thought, the No-mind before mind was born.

This is hard to understand, but as Dr. Suzuki says, 'Enlightenment consists in seeing into the meaning of life as the interplay of the relative ego with the absolute ego, In other words, enlightenment is seeing the absolute ego as reflected in the relative ego and acting through it.'* Here is the whole teaching of Buddhism on self in less than forty words. This interplay is the play of life, the dance of life, the river of life on which we flow, willingly and joyously if we are wise, clinging to the banks unavailingly if we are foolish, and suffering from our folly. For 'the mind that abides nowhere, that is our true home', and as it moves it leaves no trace; the flight of the bird of Zen is trackless and invisible. A pupil was asking the master about the Way. 'It lies before your eyes,' said the master.

'Why do I not see it for myself?'
'Because of your egoistic notion'.
'Then do you?'
'So long as you have these notions of "I" and "you", your eyes are dimmed with this relativity view.'
'Where there is neither "I" nor "you", can one see it?'
'Where there is neither "I" nor "you", who is it wants to see?'

As the centre of gravity is withdrawn from the surface, from the 'persona', through the individuality to the Essence of Mind, much happens. The personality is robbed of its strength as such. Having less weight there is less weight to be 'thrown about'. Having less pride there are less feelings to be hurt. The self can the more afford to be pushed around, to be vulnerable. Being 'nothing special' and of no importance it can afford at last to be naked to experience, to accept and absorb things as they are. Without being cold or unduly

* *Mysticism, Christian and Buddhist*, p. 47.

aloof, the man as a whole becomes more impersonal, detached from circumstance, dispassionate. As such he becomes more balanced, and hence less critical. He is a more reliable because more responsible citizen. He begins to feel and to show a greater serenity of mind, more sense of certainty with a sure sense of touch as one who has the universe behind him. He is learning to live life as it lives itself.

As for the self, the personality, it is more and more a controlled and cared-for instrument, as the piano to the musician, the car to the driver proud of his driving. Its desires and worries are less his own. There is a toothache, or a new house; a failure to become the chairman, a success on the 'Pools'. But its happiness or unhappiness are less important. For is it not right that so long as there is an 'I' at all it matters little if it be happy or unhappy? So long as there is an I to boast of its reality the man as a whole is bound in the fetters of illusion. And yet? 'Master, I would be free from illusion.' 'My son,' replied the master, 'who puts you under restraint?'

More Meditation

So much was said in an earlier chapter on Buddhist meditation that little need here be said save to point again to its necessity. How else can all these principles, many of them profoundly different from those in which we have lived a large part of our life, be built, as it were, into character? Unless some time be found each day for the cultivation of the mind, beginning with its control, and then learning to use it to spiritual ends, there will be no Zen. How can there be? To study with the intellect is easy for the western mind, but no such study leads to Zen. If the intuition is an opening bud that must be brought to flowering, it needs deliberate attention, and for this it needs long periods, short though they be at first when, secure from interruption, the mind is turned upon itself in search of that Essence of Mind which is the home of Zen. With the theme or truth set fair before it for examination, digestion and absorption, its essence seeps into the mind; then, in the daily round, it is slowly and steadily applied to all occasions, high and low, where reactions may be expected and decisions made. As for concentration, this must become a powerful weapon under command. Can the sword of Manjusri, which severs the knots of ignorance, be used effectively if it is so soft and blunt, and wobbles about so feebly in so weak a hand, that the knots are scarcely troubled in their entanglement? It must be repeated, then, that only he who can think, strongly, clearly and at will, can pass beyond thought and directly assault the citadel of Zen.

CHAPTER FIFTEEN

TRAINING FOR ZEN – III

Early Results

REGULAR meditation will bring results. It has been well said that Buddhism analyses the mind which analyses, and makes discoveries; and the deeps of the mind will react to the stimulus of the search. The results may be unpleasant, as when a pond is stirred to the bottom. There may be unwelcome psychic visions, and upsets of many kinds. There will also be pleasant 'visions', dangerous for their attraction but equally of no importance. There will be sudden 'hunches' in the course of study, an intellectual click when a missing piece of our understanding suddenly falls into place. And as the intuition develops there will be flashes of deep awareness, enabling the student to say, at least of that pebble on the shore of Truth, 'I *know*', but he will not be able to explain what it is that he knows. Somewhere in this ascending ladder of unusual experience is the first touch of Zen awareness, the fuller vision of which is Satori. Who can say when it comes? It matters not, for more will come, and when the great experience arrives it is quite unmistakable.

But with the first taste of reward may come the first call for payment. Nature preserves the balance in all things; all that is gained is paid for. The effort to climb the ladder of progress ahead of one's fellow men, and therefore ahead of the norm or normal of one's spiritual age-group, itself calls down a reaction of the stored-up Karma of the past. At any time there are accumulated effects of action awaiting adjustment in the scales of cosmic law, whether we call these consequences good or bad. He who takes his future in his hands, and moulds his own life accordingly, may be called on to pay these debts more quickly, that he may be free. He who is thus privileged will the sooner learn first-hand of that 'sea of sorrow formed of the tears of men'. Compassion has no limits, and the Bodhisattva-heart is naked to the whole world's woe. But 'joy cometh in the morning', and if, in Trine's words, we 'attach our belt to the power-house of the universe' we shall have the power of the universe to help us deal with the suffering of all mankind, and to assist each sufferer to remove that cause. This is truth, however sentimentalized. Our responsibility is infinite, *to* all that lives, *for* all that lives. If life indeed be one, each part the whole in miniature, then I *am* my brother's keeper, for I *am* my brother. His evil deeds are mine, and mine the consequence; his good deeds form a reservoir for all. This is the burden of the noblest type of Buddhist, that, in the words of *The Voice of the Silence*, he must 'remain unselfish to the endless end'.

The Middle Way between the Opposites

It has been said that the Zen path is a Middle Way with no middle. This is true, though a paradoxical way of saying it. The Buddha's Middle Way as described in his First Sermon lies between the extremes of asceticism and self-indulgence, but it is a balanced path between all pairs of opposites, not only extremes but opposing views and complementary means of ever-increasing subtlety. It has been pointed out that man walks upon two legs, moving from side to side of a median line in order to move forward. Now we must learn to see this process from, as it were, the viewpoint of the 'higher third' which embraces both, and is the hinge of the pendulum which swings between them. In time we reach a point when we see that nothing said or done is 'right', because it is partial, and therefore off the middle line. All statements are seen as one-sided, the other being in one sense equally true, and although this is baffling and confusing to the rational mind it leads one nearer to the moment of the 'unimpeded interdiffusion' of the complementary pair.

Once again let us look at the conscious and unconscious mind. Psychologically speaking we know that they 'inter-diffuse'; the newly awakening Self must learn to fuse them in a vast new consciousness. Subject and object are no longer distinct, the seer becoming the seen. The not-Self is negated more and more; the Self expands to that moment when, 'Foregoing self the universe grows I.' But this is the same thing from two points of view. The Absolute Affirmation, when the heart cries Yes to all that is, is also the final Negation, 'Neti, neti', 'not this, not this'; nothing, no thing at all, *is*. Yet the Void, the Fullness-Void consumes this pair of opposites as every other. The statements Yes and No alike are noises in the air, untrue because half true, and a realization of this truth can have a remarkable effect on all our conversation!

To the Zen practitioner, two important statements remain to be re-emphasized. First, that Prajna/Karuna, Wisdom/Compassion, are inseverable. Wisdom is useless unless and until applied in compassionate action; love must be used with wisdom as its guide or it may do harm to the beloved. And Nirvana *is* Samsara. Was ever a greater statement made in the long course of recorded history, and in the longer tradition of Wisdom not yet written down? That the Truth, Reality, the Absolute, the utmost Heaven, Nirvana itself is here and now, and to be found, and only to be found in this, the job in hand – the very thought is staggering. Here only is salvation, peace, eternal justice, all beauty, love and all the rest of the uttermost things for which we beat our fists against the bars of circumstance. He who can *know* this – what a god-like man, what a man of God, what a Master! Yet one day each of us will know it to be true, with the Knowledge that passeth understanding.

But all this lies on a Middle Way whose width is nothingness. We miss it a thousand times a day, but when for an infinite moment of no-time we walk it, wholly and free – such is a moment of Zen.

Coping with Situations

A study of the Zen Scriptures, in the sense of the collections of stories which form the basis of so many Zen sermons, will show that many of them deal with the handling of situations. Sometimes the situation is posited. The master holds up his stick. 'If you say that I have a stick you affirm; if you deny it, you negate. Speak, speak!' (i.e. say something that is neither affirmation nor denial). But in many cases the situation arose naturally, and the story appears from the right or wrong reaction of the pupil. Many of these appear in Chapter Ten on the Sayings of Zen Masters. So important is the right handling of situations that a system of Zen training might be devised on the lines of right reaction to all types of happening. To the opened eye of the master the smallest act of the pupil tells him his state of mind. How he walks or stands, or even how he sits in meditation. How he writes a single line with the brush or even, it is said, how he rings the bell outside the Master's room when entering for his moments of San-zen. All action speaks aloud to the Zen eye, and all action should be 'right' for the Zen practitioner. His response to happenings with which he is concerned should be im-mediate, impersonal, cheerful, serene, efficient for the occasion in its time and place; in brief, just right.

Each situation, large and small, from taking in the milk or posting a letter to forming a new business, is a test for the doer who claims to be a man of Zen. Indeed, I am tempted to apply the analogy of the ideal driving advocated by the Institute of Advanced Motorists in London, that a driver should be at all times driving with full concentration, yet relaxed, in the right gear at the right speed in the right traffic lane having regard to where he wants to go. And he should drive safely (with *ahimsa*, non-hurting) for himself, his passengers and the other users of the road. Should we not drive in this way in every situation, in business, in committee, round a cup of tea? The ultimate goal is higher still, that of the swordsman who has eliminated thought, and acts from No-Mind, from the springs of action behind all conscious planning. Meanwhile here are six points to consider in our reaction to any situation, as found useful in a Zen Class in London.

Give it your total attention. There is a wonderful photograph of Dr. D. T. Suzuki at 91 making tea. One feels that the whole universe is concentrated on this simple act.

Go right up to it. Face it squarely for what it is, not lying to yourself, or applying labels that you know to be untrue. If something is to be done, let it be done; whether you like it or not is quite irrelevant. Look at it, do it and drop it.

Drop the element of I. It is remarkable how many problems cease to be such when the wants of I are carefully abstracted. 'Should I do this or that?' becomes easy to answer when you remove what 'I' *want* to do. Then you see clearly what you *ought* to do. Whether you do it or not remains, of course, to be seen, but at least there is now no problem!

See that you stand on centre. This, perhaps, is a further application of going up to the problem to be faced. You cannot lift a weight just out of your reach, not a pound of it, and you will fall on your face with the effort. But stand with the two feet either side of it, and you will lift as much as your strength allows. This is part of the discipline of direct action. Why not grasp the situation, decide what is to be decided, and walk on? There are those who are ever off-centre in matters emotional and intellectual. How, then, will they reach right action in the realm of Zen?

Motive is all important. Motive decides what is 'right' or 'wrong', at least in the sense that the karma of wrong action is light indeed if the purpose of the act were good. But in Zen there is no ultimate purpose, nor any end in view. The means are the end, and each of them; the end and the means are one.

Thus the next act, even if planned as one of a series, is itself the thing to be rightly done, and im-mediately, that is, directly and now.

Then drop it. That which is done is done. It will bear its karma according as it was done. Forget it, and concentrate on the situation now. Read again the delightful story in Chapter Ten of the two monks and the pretty girl at the ford. It applies, I can assure you, to a dozen acts a day.

Everyday Life

There is an old Zen story of a monk who asked his master, 'What is Tao?' The master answered, 'Usual life is very Tao.' Here is the secret of Zen, the personal realization of the most stupendous fact in the field of human thought, that Samsara, the world of becoming, and Nirvana, the state of a mind which has attained the Absolute, are one, that 'there is nothing infinite apart from finite things', that Heaven is here and now, and nowhere else. This fact has been set out in a previous chapter, but think again. This teaching is unique in its stark simplicity. All other religions speak of a Goal to be attained, salvation to be won. Only in Mahayana Buddhism is the last dichotomy bridged and healed in the doctrine of 'Self-identity', the 'absolute interdiffusion of all particulars'. There is nowhere to go, no Path to be trodden from somewhere to anywhere else. The Relative is the expression of the Absolute which must be, therefore, Here and Now and in the doing of This. If the impact of this fact is like a knock-out blow between the eyes, reason agrees that it must be true, and the heart knows it.

But how much follows? This is far indeed from the weak assumption that it means no more than to carry on as at present, and to hope that one day somehow we shall become enlightened. This 'usual life' in Zen is a very different life, old circumstance perceived with utterly new eyes, the trivial seen as an aspect of the eternal, God in the filling of a pen. In the light of this new discovery life for the moment stops. Where are we going, then? If nowhere, why this effort, why walk on? The Answer is that we still walk on, on a Path that is trodden within, yet on steps which lie without – yet where the treading is neither in nor out but just a constant treading, just a joyful yet compassionate, relaxed yet strenuous moving with the flow of life to its own inseverable identity of every part in a living and unending whole.

What we are, therefore, what we have and have to do, is only of value as opportunity. We can afford to be content with all about us, for we made it so; in bettering it we are concerned with what we are and would be, never with what we have. Our aim is to raise the quality of living, but not necessarily the standard of living. The saint and sage are content with a hut and the simplest living, but their minds are content with nothing less than universal consciousness. Thus the present job and home and comfort is good enough; Buddhism is a ceaseless enemy to selfish ambition for the aggrandizement of self. There is nothing more important than the job in hand; there never will be, though the job may change. Zen wearies of abstractions, and always the master brings the pupil's attention back to things of here and now. 'What is the Buddha?' 'You have not finished your tea.' 'What is the nature of the ultimate Self?' 'Today I dug ten pounds of potatoes.' The former is vague, unReal and indirect. The latter is actual, natural, true.

You have your duty to perform. Do it. What could be simpler, wiser? How could anything else be true? To escape is impossible; there is no escape from the effects of causes, and present duty is presented as the karmic next thing to be done. And why try to escape? Zen can be found and will be found in doing this very duty, boring though it may seem.

All that matters in Zen is the 'moment' that is born between one and two, the moment before time itself was born. And the moment is now; it is always now but the Now as newly seen has eternal value. This when applied to the next thing to be done removes so much of our worry, and the long sequence of emotional reaction with which we plague our days. If we do not find our Satori in what we are doing because it is the right thing to do we shall never find it while doing something else. All life is changing, all the forms of it, and we flow with the river or we refuse. If we happily flow we see, as science has seen, that things are really events in time and space, that events are minor or major whirlpools on the river of time. If we flow with the river, the ceaseless tide of our karma, we can digest it, as it were, as we flow, and feel no suffering. Accept it and we are one with it; resist it and we are hurt. The false 'I' forms as we stop from flowing, and to those still moving on we shout, as a child on its sand castle, to attract admiring attention. But life has flowed on and we just look silly, while someone else must do the job we left undone. Life, then, is flow. It follows that the seeking *is* the finding, the deed is the doing of it, the means of the moment are themselves the end.

Now the lovely phrase, 'the perfume of the Void', begins to have meaning. Intangible, invisible, no 'thing', it is like a subtle air that penetrates each corner of the day. Finer in quality than any gas, it is the very essence of the smallest substance known. It dwells in all forms; it *is* the form; 'the form is emptiness, the very emptiness is form'. Yet these are the words of the Heart Sutra, at the very heart of Zen.

Then a sudden flash lifts a corner of the curtain, and consciousness is suddenly 'aware', while the hands are typing or sewing or washing up. Suddenly it is all right, all one, no difference. Thereafter usual life goes on as before, but not quite as before. Trees are once more trees, but differently seen. The wheel of rebirth still rolls, and men still suffer damnably. But it's all right now, it's all right. Karma adjusts each folly to its cause, compassion speaks and moves to heal the suffering. But it's all right; we can get on with the job in hand, which is another name for Wisdom and an excellent name for Zen.

The Ways to the One

There is a Buddhist saying, 'The Ways to the One are as many as the lives of men.' Certainly the 'devices' used by Bodhisattvas to assist humanity to its own enlightenment are all but infinite, but the duty remains on the Zen trainee to choose some method or technique and then stick to it. Only when a given form of training is honestly tried for a substantial period can it be seen to be right or wrong for that practitioner at that time. When chosen let the way be practised strenuously yet with common sense. There will be time enough to change, or to formulate and adopt a way of one's own, after long experience. And when some way is chosen and approved it is not to be viewed as necessarily the right way for any other. To dogmatize and proselytize on the virtues of one's path is to display one's own uncertainty; if it is truly the right path for that other he will be drawn to it by the excellent results on us! Yet let other roads be quietly seen. Who shall advise his friend of the right way who knows no other than his own?

In the history of Zen there are, as already described, several 'ways', such as Judo and Kendo, of which the West has heard in detail. Trevor Leggett, in his well-known essay on the subject, 'A Note on the Ways', in *A First Zen Reader*, calls them 'fractional applications of enlightenment to arts and activities in the world'. We know of Zen in the art of archery from Eugen Herrigel's book, and of the Japanese Flower Arrangement from Stella Coe, but we know most of Judo, thanks to the work of Mr. G. Koizumi, founder of the Budokwai in London, from which has sprung in forty years an International Federation of innumerable Judo clubs. But all these 'ways' have two aspects, comparable with Wisdom/Compassion. The first is technical attainment or skill in means,

and the second is the right use of it by No-mind, or in a state
of No-mind, when there is a doing but no I that does it. The
choice of the way, whether one of those developed in Japan,
or a Western equivalent, is of little importance, for he who is
well advanced in any will understand a good deal of all others.
These ways are Zen in action, exercises in the ultimate skill,
the spiritual craft of living. Be not deceived; the casual air
of the Roshi one may meet on a visit is the hall-mark of
achievement. As A. C. Graham writes in his Introduction to
the *Book of Lieh-tzu*, 'the spontaneity of Taoism and its
successor Zen is not a disruption of self-control, but an
unthinking control won, like the skill of an angler or chari-
oteer, by a long discipline.' Always, then, we come back to
self-discipline, planned and maintained by an indomitable will
to self-mastery. But tolerance must be our watchword for all
other ways. I believe that there is no such virtue as tolerance;
rather it is the progressive absence of intolerance. For intolerance of anything and anyone implies a measure of egotism
which claims to know better than anyone what is right for
someone else. As the egotism dies with the ego, so does the
intolerance. What is left is a busy minding of one's own
business, an occupation for twenty-four hours a day. For there
is no authority for such comparative excellence, nor for anything else. No master of Zen ever claims authority for Truth;
he speaks what he knows, but the other must find it to be
true. 'Even Buddhas do but point the Way.' The master
claims obedience to his method of training for so long as the
pupil agrees to try it; but when the pupil wishes to leave he
goes. And when he knows as much as the master it is the
master who sends him lightly on his way for further training.
The sole authority is the Buddha within; and no teacher,
master or book is more than a finger pointing the Way to
this Buddha, who is the Essence of Mind of you, and your
neighbour, and the man with whom you disagree. Let
the wings of the heart, then, lift and be prepared to fly.
None shall hold them, till the limit of the sky be reached,

and it has none. Let the mind abide nowhere, for that is its true home.

Holy Laughter

For the English, to be good or to be wise, or to have any clear-cut purpose in life, is to be solemn. 'This is holy; therefore you must not laugh.' This comes, of course, from the Puritan streak in all of us, and it has its value. It is the opposite of the frivolous attitude that does no single thing 'with the whole soul's will'. Zen lies between. All is important; all is of no importance at all. Nowhere is there such intensity of serious effort as in a Zen monastery; nowhere is there more genuine and joyous laughter. The spiritual life is enormous fun. Why should it not be so in the English field of Zen? If I am already Buddha, enlightened, and so are you, why should I then be sad? I suffer daily, and I see the suffering of my friends. I bear my own, as the product of my own past karma; I strive to alleviate my friends' unhappiness. For the rest, what is the value of pleasure or pain?

> Man is born many times, so he dies many times.
> Life and death continue endlessly.
> If he realizes the true meaning of unborn
> He will transcend both gladness and grief.*

The strongest enemy of laughter is fear. But the student of Zen has nothing to fear, nothing at all.

> A Zen student walks in Zen and sits in Zen.
> Whether in speech and action, or silence and inaction, his body always dwells in peace.
> He smiles, facing the sword that takes his life.
> He keeps his poise even at the moment of death.

In the light of the Unborn, which is No-mind, which is

* This verse, and those which follow, are from the Shodoka of Yoka Daishi. See Item No. 116 of *The Wisdom of Buddhism*.

without purpose or the desire for self, what do I care for the
One or the Two, for duality or Non-duality?

> Zen doctrine is no subject for sentiment.
> Doubts cannot be cleared by argument.
> I stubbornly demand your silence
> To save you from the pitfall of being and non-being.

Asked, 'What is Zen?', a master replied, 'Walk on!'

TEN PRINCIPLES OF ZEN

1. Zen, derived from the Sanskrit Dhyana, is the subject of Zen Buddhism, and connotes a state of consciousness beyond description. Zen Buddhism provides a system of training of which the immediate object is the experience known as satori. Its ultimate object is enlightenment.

2. The Zen training aims to relieve the inner tension produced by profound experience of the mind's duality. Until this problem is insufferably acute no approach to the Zen master will be profitable.

3. There are no specifically Zen Scriptures, but the doctrinal background of the training is derived from the Perfection of Wisdom Scriptures and the principles of the Yogacara School. These doctrines include Sunyata, the Void of all 'things', Tathata, the 'suchness' or essential nature of each 'thing', and Mind-only, the source of all existence, as of each human mind.

4. The experience of satori cannot be defined, for it takes place beyond the limits of concept, and out of time, in a state of non-duality before the birth of One and Two. It manifests in sudden flashes of awareness which, on the return to the plane of duality, are found to be unmistakable, impersonal and incommunicable.

5. Yet though the experience is sudden, the preparation for it is long, hard and gradual. This process cannot be hurried, yet the pressure towards achievement must be unceasing.

6. Satori cannot be achieved by the senses, the feelings or the process of thought. It can only be known through the

faculty of the intuition, the power inherent in every mind of direct, immediate perception of Reality. No one knows that he is in this condition, for in satori there is no self to know.

7. Satori is experienced in the course of daily life, though not necessarily in the present life. It is solely concerned with 'here', 'now' and 'this'. It appears as the 'No-middle' on the Middle Way between all conceivable opposites, for in the division of the opposites it has ceased to be.

8. There are degrees of enlightenment, in the depth, range and duration of the experience, but these terms have no meaning as limiting the experience itself.

9. The results of satori are not immediately visible save to the eye of the master. But its unseen effect is to raise the spiritual condition of mankind.

10. No Zen master teaches anything: there is nothing to teach, for each man is already enlightened. Yet there is a transmission of Zen.

BIBLIOGRAPHY

FOR FURTHER READING

THERE are in print some hundreds of books on Buddhism in English, and many thousands have been published in the last fifty years. The working library of the Buddhist Society alone numbers three thousand. As the field of Buddhism covers at least seven countries or cultures, with as many languages and schools of art, it is not surprising that, under the compulsion of increasing interest and ever deepening research, the number of books published every year is increasing rapidly. Here, then, is a mere selection, a hundred works being read by Western students of Buddhism today. Preference has been given to the more modern books, and to those in print. Many of these will be found in public libraries; all are available to members of the Buddhist Society, London.

(1) BASIC BUDDHISM

Arnold, Sir Edwin: *The Light of Asia.*
Conze, Edward: *Buddhism, Its Essence and Development.*
Coomaraswamy, Ananda: *Buddha and the Gospel of Buddhism.*
David-Neel, Mme A.: *Buddhism, Its Doctrines and Methods.*
Evola, J.: *The Doctrine of Awakening.*
Fussell, Ronald: *The Buddha and His Path to Self-Enlightenment.*
Holmes, Edmond: *The Creed of Buddha.*
Humphreys, Christmas:
    Buddhism (Penguin and Cassell).
    Karma and Rebirth.
    A Popular Buddhist Dictionary.
    Studies in the Middle Way.
    Walk on!
    The Way of Action.
    A Buddhist Students' Manual (Ed.).

Mehta, P: *Early Indian Religious Thought.*
Ross, Floyd: *The Meaning of Life in Hinduism and Buddhism.*
Sangharakshita, Bhikshu: *A Survey of Buddhism.*
Smith, Harold: *The Buddhist Way of Life.*
Thomas, E. J.: *The History of Buddhist Thought.*
Walters, John: *Mind Unshaken. A Modern Approach to Buddhism.*

(2) THE LIFE OF THE BUDDHA

Beck, Mrs. Adams: *The Life of the Buddha.*
Brewster, E. H.: *The Life of Gotama the Buddha.*
Thomas, E. J.: *The Life of Buddha as Legend and History.*

(3) CONCENTRATION AND MEDITATION

Conze, Edward: *Buddhist Meditation.*
Humphreys, Christmas: *Concentration and Meditation.*
Lounsbery, Constant: *Buddhist Meditation in the Southern School.*
Nyanaponika, Thera: *The Heart of Buddhist Meditation.*

(4) THE THERAVADA SCHOOL

Allen, G. F.: *The Buddha's Philosophy.*
Carus, Paul: *The Gospel of Buddha.*
Govinda, The Lama Anagarika: *The Psychological Attitude of Early Buddhist Philosophy.*
Nyantiloka, Thera: *Fundamentals of Buddhism.*
Rahula, Walpola: *What the Buddha Taught.*

(5) MAHAYANA BUDDHISM

Suzuki, Mrs. B. L.: *Mahayana Buddhism.*
Ward, C. H. S.: *Buddhism. Volume Two – Mahayana.*
Zaehner, R. C.: *The Concise Encyclopaedia of Living Faiths.* Chapter 7(b) *Buddhism. The Mahayana.* Edward Conze, Ph.D.

(6) ZEN BUDDHISM

(*a*) THE WORKS OF DR. D. T. SUZUKI:
    Essays in Zen Buddhism: First, Second, and Third Series.

The Essence of Buddhism.
Introduction to Zen Buddhism.
Manual of Zen Buddhism.
Mysticism: Christian and Buddhist.
Studies in Zen.
The Zen Doctrine of No-Mind.
Zen and Japanese Culture.

(*b*) OTHER WORKS BY JAPANESE AUTHORS:
Chisan, Koho: *Soto Zen.*
Masunaga, Reiho: *The Soto Approach to Zen.*
Ogata, Sohaku: *Zen for the West.*
Senzaki and McCandless: *Buddhism and Zen.*

(*c*) CH'AN BUDDHISM
Chang, Chen-chi: *The Practice of Zen.*
Luk, Charles: *Ch'an and Zen Teaching*: Series One, Two, and
Three.

(*d*) LIFE IN A ZEN MONASTERY:
Aitken, Robert: *Zen Training, a Personal Account* (Paper).
Herrigel, Eugen: *The Method of Zen.*
De Martino, Richard:
Essay, 'The Human Situation and Zen Buddhism' in
Fromm, Suzuki and de Martino: *Zen Buddhism and
Psycho-analysis.*
Sasaki, Ruth Fuller: *Rinzai Zen Study for Foreigners in Japan*
(Paper).

(*e*) WESTERN WRITERS ON ZEN
Benoit, Hubert: *The Supreme Doctrine.*
Blyth, R. H.: *Zen in English Literature.*
Dumoulin and Sasaki: *The Development of Chinese Zen.*
Durckheim, Karlfried Graf von: *The Japanese Cult of
Tranquillity.*
Gabb, W. J.: *The Goose is Out.*
Harding, D. E.: *On Having No Head* (Paper).
Herrigel, Eugen: *Zen in the Art of Archery.*
Humphreys, Christmas:
Zen Buddhism.
Zen Comes West.

Leggett, Trevor: *A First Zen Reader* (Ed.).
Linssen, Robert: *Living Zen.*
Powell, Robert: *Zen and Reality.*
Watts, Alan:
    The Spirit of Zen.
    The Way of Zen.
Wei Wu Wei:
    Fingers Pointing Towards the Moon.
    Why Lazarus Laughed.

(7) TIBETAN BUDDHISM

David-Neel and Yongden: *The Secret Oral Teaching in Tibetan Buddhist Sects.*
Govinda, the Lama Anagarika: *Foundations of Tibetan Mysticism.*
Guenther, H.: *The Jewel Ornament of Liberation.*
Norbu and Harrer: *Tibet is My Country.*
Pallis, Marco: *Peaks and Lamas.*

(8) BUDDHISM IN FICTION

Beck, Mrs. Adams: *The Garden of Vision.*
Mundy, Talbot: *Om.*
Payne, Robert: *The Lord Comes.*
Thompson, Edward: *The Youngest Disciple.*
Yongden, Lama: *Mipam.*

(9) SCRIPTURES

General Anthologies:
    Conze, E.: *Buddhist Scriptures* (Penguin).
    Conze, E.: *Buddhists Texts Through the Ages.*
    Humphreys, Christmas: *The Wisdom of Buddhism.*

Theravada:
    The Dhammapada: Many Translations.
    Nyantiloka, Thera: *The Word of the Buddha.*
    Warren, H. C.: *Buddhism in Translations.*
    Woodward, F. L.: *Some Sayings of the Buddha.*

BIBLIOGRAPHY

Mahayana:

Blavatsky, H. P.: *The Voice of the Silence* (Trans.).

Conze, E.:

Buddhist Wisdom Books.

Selected Sayings from the Perfection of Wisdom.

Zen School:

The Mumonkan: As Appendix 'A' in Ogata, Sohaku, *Zen for the West.*

The Blue Cliff Records (The Hekigan Roku): Trans. R. D. M. Shaw.

The Sutra of Hui-neng (Wei Lang): Trans. Wong Mou-lam.

The Zen Teaching of Huang-Po: Trans. Blofeld.

The Iron Flute: Trans. Senzaki and McCandless.

See also:

The Tao Te Ching: Trans. Ch'u Ta-kao.

Chuang Tzu: Trans. Herbert A. Giles.

The Secret of the Golden Flower: Wilhelm and Jung.

GLOSSARY

of Zen terms mentioned in this work, or which will be found in Zen literature in English. For other Buddhist terms see the larger Glossary in *A Buddhist Students' Manual*, published by the Buddhist Society in London, or for greater detail *A Popular Buddhist Dictionary*, edited by Christmas Humphreys, published by the Arco Press.

ABBREVIATIONS

Bsm.	-	Buddhism
Bst.	-	Buddhist
Chin.	-	Chinese
Cp.	-	Compare
E.g.	-	For example
Jap.	-	Japanese
Lit.	-	Literally
M.	-	Mahayana
P.	-	Pali
q.v.	-	Which see
Sk.	-	Sanskrit

W. of Bsm. *The Wisdom of Buddhism*. Ed. Christmas Humphreys.

Bodhi (Sk.) Enlightenment. The spiritual condition of a Buddha or Bodhisattva. The cause of *Bodhi* is *Prajñā* (q.v.) wisdom, and Karunā (q.v.) compassion. (*See* **Buddhi.**)

Bodhidharma (Sk.) Indian Bst. who arrived at the Chinese Court in A.D. 520. Known in China as Tamo, and in Japan as Daruma. For his famous interview with the Emperor *see W. of Bsm. No. 118.* The twenty-eighth Indian and first Chinese Zen Patriarch. (*See* **Patriarchs.**) The father of Zen Bsm., although it was left to

Masters of the eighth century, led by Hui-neng, to consolidate his teaching and technique into a school of Bsm.

Bodhisattva (Sk.) Bodhisatta (P.) One whose 'being' or 'essence' (*sattva*) is *bodhi*, that is, the wisdom resulting from direct perception of Truth, with the compassion awakened thereby.

In Theravāda, an aspirant for Buddha-hood. In Mahāyāna, the Bodhisattva is the ideal of the Path as contrasted with the Arhat of the Theravāda. Having practised the Six Paramitas and attained Enlightenment, he renounces Nirvāna in order to help humanity on its pilgrimage.

Buddhi (Sk.) The vehicle of Enlightenment (*Bodhi*, q.v.). The faculty of supreme understanding as distinct from the understanding itself. The sixth principle in the sevenfold constitution of man taught in the esoteric schools of Buddhism, and as such the link between the Ultimate Reality and the Mind (*Manas*). Nearest English equivalent is the intuition.

Ch'an (Chin.) From the Sk. Dhyāna. In Jap., Zen. The Zen Bsm. of Japan derives from the Ch'an Bsm. of China, founded in the sixth century by Bodhidharma.

Cha-no-yu (Jap.) The Japanese Tea Ceremony. Lit. Tea and hot water. The ceremonial making and taking of tea in a mood which aims at *Satori* (q.v.). A form of Japanese culture which springs from Zen Buddhism.

Dharmakāya (Sk.) The Body of the Law. The Buddha as the personification of Truth. The Essence Body, 'Consciousness merged in the Universal Consciousness'.

Dhyāna (Sk.); P., Jhāna; Chin. Ch'an (q.v.); Jap. Zen. A term so fundamental in Bsm. that the above variations have four distinguishable meanings. Basic meaning, meditation. The practice of Dhyāna leads to Samādhi (q.v.); both are to be distinguished from Prajñā (q.v.) which is out of time and duality. Rinzai Zen, following Hui-neng, concentrates on Prajñā; Sōtō on Dhyāna, quiet meditation, though both are necessary.

Diamond Sutra The Vajracchedikā Prajñāpāramitā Sutra, 'the Perfection of Wisdom which cuts like a Diamond'. One of the two most famous Scriptures in the vast Perfection of Wisdom (Prajñā-pāramitā) group of the Mahāyāna Scriptures. The Heart Sutra (q.v.) is a still smaller epitome of this 'Wisdom which has gone beyond'.

Dōgen (Jap.)   The Japanese Founder of Sōtō Zen Bsm. in Japan (1200–1253). Dōgen studied the teaching of the T'saotung School in China for four years before bringing it, in 1227, to Japan. He stands alone as the Founder of the Japanese School, and is by far its greatest name. He would have no dealings with the Court, but retired to the mountains where he founded Eiheiji, near Fujui. There he taught that moral training, meditation and enlightenment are three facets of one process. Dōgen was a very great man, and his school of Zen Bsm. should be far better known.

Dōjō (Jap.)   Any place where Bst. teaching is given or the Way practised. Hence a Bst. monastery, but used more particularly in Jūdō (q.v.) and Kendō (q.v.) for the room where that art is practised. Cp. *Sōdō*.

Ekacitta (Sk.)   The 'one thought-moment' out of time, in which the Zen monk experiences Non-duality, that state before the One became the Many, before thought was born. Cp. *Ichinen, Kenshō, Satori*.

Engakuji (Jap.)   Famous Rinzai Zen monastery in Kamakura, founded in 1282 by Hōjō Tokimune for his Zen teacher, Bukkō Kokushi, who became the first Abbot.

Goroku (Jap.)   Enigmatic remarks or replies by Zen masters to their pupils, often collected into such works at the *Mumonkan* or *Hekigan Roku* for the use of later generations.

Gradual School of Enlightenment   The Zen School of Shen-Hsiu, pupil of Hung-jen, the Fifth Chinese Zen Patriarch, who founded this School in the North while Hui-neng (q.v.) founded the Sudden School in the South.

Hakuin, Ekaku (Jap.)   Hakuin Zenji, the Zen teacher (1685–1768), was the father of purely Japanese Rinzai Zen Bsm., as distinct from Chinese Ch'an Bsm. practised in Japan. He believed in fierce, direct methods of training, and entirely remodelled the Kōan system. He trained a large number of successors. A prolific writer, little of his work is yet published in English.

Heart Sutra, The   The Prajñāpāramitā Hridaya Sutra, one of the smallest and, with the Diamond Sutra (q.v.) the most popular of the many Scriptures contained in the vast Prajñā-pāramitā literature. As the Shingyō it is recited daily in countless Bst. monasteries in Japan.

Hondō (Jap.)   The main hall, usually a separate building, in a Jap. monastery, used principally for lectures and meals. The image in it is usually that of the Founder. Cp. *Zen-dō.*

Hossu (Jap.)   Short stick carried by Zen masters. Originally a fly whisk, with a tuft of horse-tail at the end, it became a religious instrument used in ceremonies. Cp. *Keisaku, Shippei.*

Hsin (Chin.)   In Japanese Shin or Kokoro. A key term in Zen Bsm. Mind or heart, but not in Western sense of either term. The deepest aspects of both; inmost heart or deepest mind; soul but without that term's theological implications. That factor in each human being which is part of All-Mind.

Hsu Yün   Chinese Ch'an master who died in Kiangsi, China, in 1959 at the age of 120. Recognized as the successor to all the 'Five Houses' of Ch'an Bsm. A few of his sermons appear in Chang Chen-chi, *The Practice of Zen* (1959) and more in Luk, *Ch'an and Zen Teaching* (1960).

Huang-Po (Chin.)   In Jap. Ōbaku: *d.* 850. A pupil two generations removed from the sixth Patriarch, Hui-neng, Huang-Po was the Zen master of Rinzai. Some of Huang-Po's teaching was recorded by P'ei Hsiu as *The Zen Teaching of Huang-Po on the Transmission of Mind,* for which see trans. by John Blofeld, 1958.

Hua Tou (Chin.)   Lit. a word's end. A shortened version of the Kō-an (q.v.), in that a fragment only of the story or situation is used for this form of Zen meditation.

Hui-neng (Chin.)   In Canton dialect, Wei-lang. In Jap, Enō (637–713). The Sixth Patriarch of Chinese Zen Bsm., the virtual founder of Ch'an (Zen) Bsm. as a School of its own. His was the 'Sudden' school as distinct from the 'Gradual' school of Shen-hsiu (q.v.), which soon died out, but both the Rinzai and Sōtō branches of Hui-neng's School have flourished for a thousand years. Hui-neng was the last Zen Patriarch, though many famous Zen Masters followed him. For a trans. by Wong Mou-lam of the Tan Ching, the Platform Sutra of the Patriarch, *see* the *Sutra of Wei Lang* (*Hui-neng*) (1944).

Hung-jen (Chin.) In Jap. Gunin (605–675). The fifth Chinese Zen Patriarch. He had, it is said, 500 disciples, the most famous being Shen-hsiu and Hui-neng (q.v.).

Ichinen (Jap.) A term of Zen Bsm. Lit. One thought, or mental event. When this first happens the mind is said to be 'disturbed,' and there arises an awareness of duality, of true and untrue, good and evil. A mind which can revert to the state of No-Mind, before this 'disturbance' takes place, is free from the anxiety, fear and desire which all thought produces. Cp. *Ekacitta*.

I-ching (Chin.) The 'great spirit of inquiry', the 'perpetual knocking at a door' (Suzuki) which is necessary before the break-through to Satori is attained. The word 'doubt' is too negative, for the state of mind is also fiercely positive. Not to be confused with the Chinese classic, *I Ching* ('Book of Changes').

Intuition The faculty in the mind of im-mediate knowledge as distinct from the intellect which can never know more than 'about it and about'. It has been described as knowing without knowing how you know. The Bst. equivalent is Buddhi (q.v.) which, how-ever, has a 'higher intellectual' content.

Ji (Jap.) (1) A suffix to a name, meaning temple-monastery. Thus Engaku-ji at Kamakura. The suffix -In has the same meaning, as in Chion-in, the mother temple of the Jōdo sect. The suffix -An means a smaller temple within a larger unit, as in Shōden-an, Dr. Suzuki's house in Engaku-ji.

(2) (also pronounced Shi), teacher, as Hakuin Zen-ji, the Zen teacher.

(3) A fact, event, object, particular thing; the opposite to Ri, which means principles, rather as spiritual principles. (*See* **Jijimuge**.)

Jijimuge (Jap.) The unimpeded interdiffusion (*muge*) of all Ji meaning things, facts, objects. The summit of intellectual under-standing of the non-duality of manifestation. The 'Thou art THAT' of Hindu philosophy still admits three things to be One; Jijimuge is beyond even Unity. The supreme teaching of the Kegon School of Japanese Bsm.

Jikijitsu (Jap.) The leader of Zazen in the Zendō of a Rinzai Zen monastery. He is in charge of the meditation in the Zendō, keeps time with the clappers and gong, leads recitations and keeps discipline. The most important official after the Rōshi. Cp. *Jisha*.

Jiriki (Jap.) Salvation through one's own efforts, as opposed to *Tariki*, salvation through the efforts of Another. All Japanese sects are attributable to one of these two divisions.

Jisha (Jap.) An important official in a Zen temple. With the Jikijitsu (q.v.) he handles all Zendō affairs. He keeps the Zendō clean, helps newcomers, serves tea, and reports regularly to the Rōshi. He is the administrative as distinct from the training official in the Zendō life.

Jūdō (Jap.) First known as Jū-jutsu, this Japanese form of wrestling applies the principles of Taoism and Zen to physical contest. Victory is gained by giving way, and the attacker's strength is used to his own undoing (cp. *Kendō*).

Jūshoku (Jap.) The head monk of a Zen temple. Also used for the incumbent or 'parish priest' of a small temple.

Kanchō (Jap.) The Abbot of a monastery. The administrative head, who may or may not act as Rōshi (q.v.).

Karma (Sk.) **Kamma** (P.) Root meaning 'Action'; derived meaning 'action and the appropriate result of action'; the law of cause and effect. As applied to the moral sphere it is the Law of ethical Causation, through the operation of which a man 'reaps what he sows', builds his character, makes his destiny, and works out his salvation.

Karunā (Sk.) Active compassion. One of the 'two pillars' of Mahayana Bsm., the other being *Prajñā* (q.v.). One of the Four *Brahma Vihāras* or Divine States resulting from the elimination of selfish inclinations. (*See* **Bodhisattva**.)

Keisaku (Jap.) A light flat stick, representing the sword of Manjusri, used by a senior monk in the Zen-dō (q.v.) to rouse monks falling asleep or, at invitation, to smack shoulder muscles grown stiff from sitting.

Kendō (Jap.) The Japanese form of fencing. A two-handed sword is used, of bamboo strips lightly bound in leather.

Kenshō (Jap.) 'Seeing into one's own nature', the goal of Zen practice. The first experience of Satori (q.v.).

Kinhin (Jap.) 'Sutra-walking.' Formal marching round the Zen-dō of a Zen monastery during periods of rest from Za-Zen meditation, to loosen stiff joints and exercise the body.

Kō-an (Jap.) From the Chin. Kung-an, a public document. A technical term in Rinzai Zen Bsm. A word or phrase of nonsensical language which cannot be 'solved' by the intellect but which holds its attention while a higher faculty takes over. Used as an exercise for breaking the limitations of thought and developing the intuition (q.v.), thereby attaining a flash of awareness beyond duality (Kenshō), and in due course Satori (q.v.). This exercise, and its companion the Mondō, is not used in Sōtō Zen.

Kokushi (Jap.) A title given to a great teacher in Japan by the Emperor of the day, meaning National Teacher, e.g. Daitō Kokushi, the posthumous title of Daitō, a great Zen master of the fourteenth century, and founder of Daitokuji.

Koromo (Jap.) The black or dark blue robe worn by a Japanese monk over which he wears the Kesa or distinguishing garment of his Shū or Bst. School.

Kyō (Jap.) A suffix to a name, meaning scripture. Thus Koke-kyō, the Jap. for the Saddharma-pundarīka Sūtra. For euphony it may become 'gyō'.

Mahāyāna The School of the Great Vehicle (of salvation), also called the Northern School as it embraces Tibet, Mongolia, China, Korea and Japan. Cp. *Theravāda*. The Mahāyāna gradually developed from the primitive teaching, and no sharp line of demarcation has ever existed. The teaching of the M. is more distinctly religious, making its appeal to the heart and intuition rather than to the intellect. It seeks the spiritual interpretation of the verbal teaching.

and endeavours to expound that teaching in a variety of forms calculated to appeal to every type of mind and every stage of spiritual development.

Middle Way, The (1) The Majjhima Patipadā or Middle Way described by the Buddha in his First Sermon. It is the Noble Eightfold Path between all extremes which leads to Enlightenment. *See* W. of Bsm. No. 13. (2) The name of the Journal of the Buddhist Society of London which was called, until 1943, *Buddhism in England*. (3) The Mādhyamika, the Middle Way School founded by Nāgārjuna in the second century A.D.

Mokugyo (Jap.) Lit. a wooden fish. The wooden drum hollowed from a block, used in Zen Bst. monasteries to call the monks to a service or to accompany Sutra chanting.

Mondō (Jap.) 'Questions and answers.' The short, pithy dialogues between Zen masters and their disciples. The bulk of Zen literature consists of these *mondō* and commentaries upon them. Some of the answers may be used as a *Kō-an* (q.v.).

Mu (Jap.) In Chinese, Wu. Not, or No, the Negative which is beyond mere positive and negative. (*See*, e.g. **No-Mind**.)

Nirvāna (Sk.) **Nibbāna** (P.) The supreme Goal of Buddhist endeavour; release from the limitations of existence. The word is derived from a root meaning extinguished through lack of fuel, and since rebirth is the result of desire (*tanhā*), freedom from rebirth is attained by the extinguishing of all such desire. Nirvāna is, therefore, a state attainable in this life by right aspiration, purity of life, and the elimination of egoism.

Nō (Jap.) Lit. Performance. The Nō plays of Japan date from seventh century. Many have a Bst. theme. The action and manner of dancing and of speech became highly stylized, and today the art is a cult of the few learned enough to understand the symbolic meaning.

No-Mind Phrase used to translate various terms in Ch'an and Zen Bsm. It describes a state of consciousness before the division into duality created by thought takes place. Wu-hsin (in Jap. Mu-shin) means no-mindness, or no-thoughtness, as the Unconscious behind all conscious activity. Yet this Unconscious is at the same time conscious, a mind unconscious of itself.

Ogata, Sōhaku Japanese Bst., born 1901. Chief Monk of Chōtoku-in, a sub-temple of Shōkokuji, a Rinzai Zen monastery in Kyoto. Has for thirty years assisted Western students of Zen in their studies in Japan, as host, interpreter, teacher and friend. Has studied and taught in Chicago University. Visited England in 1957 as guest of the Buddhist Society, London. Author of *A Guide to Zen Practice* (1923) and *Zen for the West* (1959).

Patriarchs The Zen School of China and Japan claims a line of twenty-eight Patriarchs beginning with the Buddha himself and passing through many famous names, such as Asvaghosha, Nāgārjuna and Vasubandhu to Bodhidharma of India, who was the twenty-eighth Indian and first Chinese Zen Patriarch. The six Chinese Patriarchs were (1) Bodhidharma (Ch. Tamo, Jap. Daruma) who reached China in 520, (2) Hui-k'o (Jap. Eka) 486–593, (3) Seng-t'san (Jap. Sosan) died 606, (4) Tao-hsin (Jap. Dōshin) 579–651, (5) Hung-jen (Jap. Gunin) 601–675, and (6) Hui-neng (Jap. Enō or Yenō) 637–713, who left no successor as Patriarch.

Prajñā (Sk.) **Paññā** (P.) Transcendental wisdom, divine intuition. One of the two pillars of the M., the other being *Karunā* (q.v.). For comparison with *Dhyāna, see* Suzuki, *Living by Zen,* Ch. V, *and* Suzuki, *The Zen Doctrine of No-Mind,* pp. 95–97.

Prajñā-pāramitā (Sk.) The literature known generally as the Prajñā-pāramitā (the 'Wisdom which has gone beyond') was compiled in India over many centuries, beginning in the first century B.C. The two most famous epitomes are the *Diamond Sutra* (q.v.) and the *Heart Sutra* (q.v.), both of the fourth century A.D.

Prānayāma (Sk.) Breath-control.

Rebirth An Indian doctrine which the Buddha embodied in his own teaching in a modified form. To be distinguished from transmigration, for the latter implies the return to earth in a new body of a distinct entity which may be called a soul. In Bsm. Rebirth is the corollary of *Karma* (q.v.); i.e. no immortal entity passes from life to life, but each life must be considered the karmic effect of the previous life and the cause of the following life. The *karma* which causes man to return to this world in a cycle of rebirths is the result of desire.

Rinzai School of Zen Buddhism Founded by Rinzai. (Chin. Lin-Chi) and taken to Japan by Eisai in 1190. This School of Zen became known to the West through the work of Dr. D. T. Suzuki. (Cp. Sōtō Zen.) The Kōan and Mondō are used in Rinzai Zen but very little in Sōtō Zen.

Rōshi (Jap.) Lit. The old teacher. Rōshi is the name given to the Zen master of a monastery who takes the pupil-monks and laymen in San-Zen and gives them Zen instruction. He may be at the same time the Abbot, but in large monasteries the two offices are frequently distinct, the Abbot concentrating on administration while the Rōshi confines himself to practical instruction in Zen.

Ryōsen-an A sub-temple of Daitokuji at Kyoto, Japan, re-founded by Mrs. Ruth Sasaki (q.v.) as a training centre for Western Zen students. At the formal opening in 1958 Mrs. Sasaki was given the title of Jūshoku or head-priest, an honour never before accorded a Westerner or a woman.

Samādhi (Sk. and P.) Contemplation on Reality, the state of even-mindedness when the dualism caused by thought has ceased to ruffle the surface of the ocean of Truth. In it the distinction between the mind, the object and their relationship is transcended. Sammā Samādhi is the last step on the Noble Eightfold Path and a prelude to Nirvāna. But the final step is a large one, from duality to Non-duality. (*See* **Dhyāna, Prajñā, Satori.**)

Samsāra (Sk. and P.) Also spelt Sangsāra. Lit. Faring on, a stream (of becoming). The world of flux, change and ceaseless becoming in which we live. Daily life. In Bsm. the field of deliverance from its bondage of limitation; there is none other. The purpose of the Noble Eightfold Path is to enable one to step off the Wheel, into the state of Nirvāna (q.v.). But in the M. School it is taught that no such escape is truly possible, for Samsāra and Nirvāna are two aspects of one Reality; they are an inseverable, twofold aspect of the ultimate Non-duality.

Samurai (Jap.) The Japanese warrior who, imbued with the spirit of Bushido, the 'Way to Knightly Virtue', was trained mentally and physically to apply, in the service of his Lord or Emperor, the highest principles of bravery, chivalry, honour and contempt for death.

San-Zen (Jap.) Tense interview between a Rōshi, or Rinzai Zen master, and a monk or layman under Zen training. Subject is usually the Kōan, on which the student is then engaged. Interview may take seconds or minutes. May take place daily or several times a day. (*See* **Sesshin**) San-Zen is the heart of the Rinzai Zen training.

Sasaki, Mrs. Ruth Fuller American Zen Buddhist, widow of Sōkei-an Sasaki. Now 'chief monk' of Ryōsen-an, a sub-temple of Daitokuji, Kyoto, rebuilt in its grounds under her auspices for Western students of Zen. The first Western Bst. to be given this or any rank in Zen Bsm.

Satori (Jap.) In Chin., Wu. A technical term used in Zen Bsm. to describe a state of consciousness beyond the plane of discrimination and differentiation. It may vary in quality and duration from a flash of intuitive awareness to Nirvāna. It is the beginning and not the end of true Zen training. After this 'break-through' to No-Thought, or No-Mind (q.v.), there is a period of maturing and then the rebuilding of the whole man in the light of this direct experience of Non-Duality. In Rinzai Zen the Kōan and Mondō (q.v.) are used to achieve Satori; in Sōtō Zen (q.v.) they are used very rarely. In either event the experience itself is unmistakable and incommunicable. (*See* **Enlightenment, Kenshō.**)

Seng-t'san (Chin.) In Jap., Sosan. *d.* 606. The third Chinese Zen Patriarch, famous for his long poem 'On Trust in the Heart'. *See* W. of Dsm., No. 111.

Sesshin (Jap.) Period of intensive meditation in a Rinzai Zen monastery, sometimes lasting a week, during which the monks sit in meditation for a large proportion of the day and night with frequent visits to the Rōshi (q.v.) for San-Zen (q.v.).

Shippei (Jap.) A stick on which a Zen master supports himself and uses to deliver blows. Cp. *Hossu, Keisaku.*

Shōbōgenzō (Jap.) 'The Eye of the True Law.' One of the most famous works of Dōgen (q.v.) the Founder of Sōtō Zen in Japan.

See Masunaga, *The Soto Approach to Zen*, for partial translation. (*See* Sōtō.)

Shu (Jap.)   A school or sub-division of a larger School of Japanese Bsm. Thus, the Shin-Shū or Zen-Shū.

Sōdō (Jap.)   The training school for monks in a Zen monastery. It has its Zendō (q.v.) where the monks meditate by day and sleep by night, and quarters for the Rōshi, the Zen teacher. It has its terms like any other school.

Sōtō (Jap.)   The Sōtō Zen School of Japanese Bsm. was founded by Dōgen (q.v.), who brought the Chinese Tsao-tung School to Japan in 1127. Teaching descended from Hui-neng through Tōsan and Wanshi, as did Rinzai Zen through Huang Po (Ōbaku) and Rinzai (Lin-chi) and Eisai, who brought it to Japan in the same period. Sōtō relies on Shikan Taza, deep meditation, rather than the 'sudden' methods with Kōan and Mondō of Rinzai, which concentrates on prajñā, Wisdom, and its direct attainment. Sōtō aims at repentance, then moral training, then meditation in the light of the Enlightenment which already exists within. The three, meditation, moral training and Enlightenment are facets of one process. We should live 'as if' we were what we are, enlightened Buddhas. 'Life is the active expression of Buddha at work', and we should act accordingly. The mother temples of the two branches are Eiheiji, near Fukui, and Sōjiji at the back of Yokohama.

Suzuki, Daisetz Teitaro, LITT.D.(OTANI UNIV.)   Japanese philosopher and writer, born 18th October, 1870, of a Rinzai Zen family. While at Imperial Univ. Tokyo studied Zen at Kama-kura under the Rōshi Imagita Kosen. On the death of the Rōshi studied under his successor, Sōyen Shaku (author of *Sermons of a Buddhist Abbot* (1906), and under him gained his enlightenment. Author of a score of major works in English, ten in Japanese, and innumerable articles, nearly all on Zen Buddhism, attempting to explain its history, nature and importance to the Western world.

Tan (Jap.)   The raised platform round the sides of the Zen-dō (q.v.) of a Zen monastery covered with *tatami*, straw mats, on which the monks meditate by day and sleep by night.

Tatami (Jap.)   The thick straw mats which cover the floor of a

Japanese room. Of standard size, 6 feet by 3 feet, they are used for the measurement of a room. As the users of such a room sit on cushions on the floor, shoes are removed on entering.

Tathāgata (Sk.) A title of the Buddha, used by his followers, and also by himself when speaking of himself. Derivation doubtful, but usually derived from *tathā-āgata* (thus come), or *tathā-gata* (thus gone), and given the meaning 'He who has come and gone as former Buddhas': i.e. teaching the same truths, and following the same Path to the same Goal.

Tathatā (Sk.) Lit. 'Thusness' or 'Suchness'. Term used in Mahāyāna for the ultimate and unconditioned nature of all things. In one sense it is *Sūnya* expressed positively. It is that which is expressed in all separate things, which is not different from them and which is not divided by them. It cannot be called the One as distinct from the Many, for it is not distinct from anything. Nothing can be denied or affirmed concerning it, for these are modes of expression which exclude and thereby create opposition. It can only be understood by realizing that one can neither find it by searching nor lose it by trying to separate oneself from it. Yet it has to be found. Cp. *Dharmakāya*.

Theravāda The 'Doctrine of the Elders' who formed the first Buddhist Council. The sole survivor of the 18 sects into which by the third century B.C. the original Hīnayāna School of Bsm. was divided. Until recently this school was known in the West by its generic name of Hīnayāna, which means small or lesser vehicle (of salvation), but this term of reproach, coined by the Mahāyānists, has now been dropped in favour of the more accurate and less discourteous name of *Theravāda*, the Way of the Elders. (*See* **Mahāyāna**.)

Tokonoma (Jap.) The alcove in the principal room of a Japanese house, once a shrine for some deity and still a shrine for beauty. Only a single picture and a single vase with one or two blooms will be found therein, but these will be as perfect as the owner's purse and taste allow.

Usual Life The Zen master Jōshu, when asked, 'What is Tao?' replied, 'Your every-day life.' This has been interpreted by some to mean that if we just live our usual life we shall gain Enlightenment.

This is not the meaning. It means that we shall not find Enlightenment by a study of scriptures and meditation alone, but by a suddenly acquired awareness that this daily life *is* the Absolute in action and *is* Nirvāna itself, if only it can be seen with the new eyes of enlightenment. To achieve this new vision is the purpose of Zen training.

Walk on!   (1) A phrase used first by the Zen master Ummon who, when asked 'What is Tao?' replied, 'Walk on!' Since used to symbolize the 'direct' approach of Zen Bsm. to Reality. (2) The name of a book by Christmas Humphreys (1956).

Za-Zen (Jap.) 'Zen-sitting.' Zen meditation, usually in the Zen-dō (q.v.). The correct posture is 'the Lotus posture', in which the sole of each foot is upturned on the opposite thigh. The subject in Rinzai Zen monasteries is usually the Kōan (q.v.) given by the Rōshi or Zen master to that pupil. (*See* **Mondō, Sesshin.**)

Zen-dō (Jap.)   The hall, usually a separate building, used in a Zen monastery for Za-Zen, meditation. The monks have each a mat (*Tatami*), 6 feet by 3 feet, on which to sit, and they sleep on it at night. The mats are on a platform (*Tan*) on two sides of the Zen-dō, with a wide space in between. For photographs of a Zen-dō in use *see* Suzuki, *Zen and Japanese Buddhism*.

Zen-ji (Jap.)   A teacher of Zen, as Hakuin Zen-ji, the Zen teacher Hakuin. Cp. *Ji* (1) and (3).

INDEX

INDEX

Abbot (of monastery). *See* Kancho.
Abegg, Lily, 64
Abhidhamma, 67
Absolute, the, 7, 49, 60, 117, 122, 123, 124, 160, 163
Abstractions, Zen attitude to, 97, 116, 153, 164
Acceptance, 118
ahimsa (no-harm), 34, 59, 162
Alaya-Vijnana, 67
anatta, 27, 28, 30, 31, 56
anicca (change), 27, 28, 31
Archery, 106, 131
Arhat, 48, 60–64
Arnold, Sir Edwin; quoted, 22–23
Astrology, 145
Aurelius, Marcus, 36–37
Avalokita, 70
avidya (ignorance), 62

Basho, 117
'Beat' Zen, 9, 82, 107, 136–7
Benoit, Dr. Hubert, 131
   Supreme Doctrine, The, 142
Bhagavad Gita, 25, 101
Bhakti Yoga, 21, 133
Bhikkhu, 19, 26, 58, 83
Blake, William, quoted, 152
Blavatsky, H. P., quoted, 37
Blue Cliff Records (Hekigan Roku), 85, 105
Blyth, R. H., 8, 117, 130; quoted, 24
   Zen in English Literature, 8, 130
Bodhi (wisdom), 62, 179. *See also Buddhi;* Enlightenment.
Bodhidharma (Daruma, Tamo), 10, 82–84, 86, 87, 108–9, 116, 119, 121–2, 151, 179
Bodhisattva, 17, 49, 60, 62–64, 70–77, 108, 125, 159, 166, 180
Bodhisattva Vow, the, 135, 144

Bodhi-tree, the, 32, 88
Book of Lieh-tzu, 167
Brahma Viharas, the Four, 48–49
Brooke, Rupert, quoted, 100
Brussels, 131
Buddha, the, 5, 17–19, 22, 26, 27, 30, 32, 56, 59, 61, 69, 71–76, 78, 81, 86, 107, 111, 149, 152, 159, 167
   First Sermon of, 159
Buddhi, 21, 144, 180
Buddhism (C. Humphreys), 57, 81
Buddhist Society, the, 112, 173
Budokwai, 166
Burma, 26, 44, 55

Calligraphy, 106
Cambodia, 26, 55
Ceylon, 26, 55
Ch'an, 7, 43, 81, 82, 87, 91, 131, 180
Chang Chen-Chi, 131
Cha-no-yu, 180
Chi, Dr. Richard, 121
China, the Chinese, 7, 10, 55, 81ff., 105, 115, 121, 130–1, 138, 151
Ch'ung-yuan, 74
Coe, Stella, 106, 166
Communication, failures in, 93–94
Compassion. *See* Karuna.
Concentration, 27, 46, 47, 50
Concentration and Meditation (Pub. Buddhist Society), 45, 46
Confucius, 82, 86
Contemplation, 50
Conze, Dr. Edward, 65, 69

Daitoku-ji, 104
Daruma. *See* Bodhidharma.
Deva planes, 124
Development of Chinese Zen, The (Dumoulin), 91

195